DOE/EA-1775

FINAL ENVIRONMENTAL ASSESSMENT

FOR THE

TEXAS A&M UNIVERSITY COMBINED HEAT AND POWER PROJECT, COLLEGE STATION, TEXAS

U.S. Department of Energy
National Energy Technology Laboratory

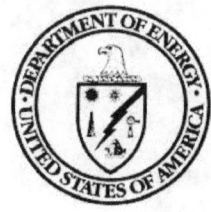 

September 2010

COVER SHEET

Responsible Agency: U.S. Department of Energy (DOE)

Title: *Final Environmental Assessment for the Texas A&M Combined Heat and Power Project, College Station, Texas* (DOE/EA-1775)

Contact: For additional copies or more information about this environmental assessment (EA), please contact:

> Mr. Bill Gwilliam
> U.S. Department of Energy
> National Energy Technology Laboratory
> P.O. Box 880, MS B07
> 3610 Collins Ferry Road
> Morgantown, West Virginia 26507-0880
> Facsimile: (304) 285-4403
> E-mail: william.gwilliam@netl.doe.gov

Abstract: DOE prepared this Environmental Assessment (EA) to evaluate the potential environmental consequences of providing a financial assistance grant under the American Recovery and Reinvestment Act of 2009 to Texas A&M University (Texas A&M) for installation of a combined heat and power (CHP) system at its campus in College Station, Texas.

DOE's proposed action is to provide $10 million in financial assistance in a cost-sharing arrangement with the project proponent, Texas A&M. The cost of the proposed project would be about $70.3 million. Texas A&M's proposed project is to install and operate a high-efficiency CHP system that would produce steam for heating and cooling as well as generate electricity. This EA evaluates commonly addressed environmental resource areas and identifies no significant adverse environmental impacts for the proposed project. The proposed project would upgrade the Central Utility Plant and campus electrical distribution system to serve Texas A&M expansion. The proposed CHP system would result in substantial energy savings, reduce carbon dioxide emissions, and reduce the amount of electricity Texas A&M would purchase from carbon-producing plants such coal-fired power generators.

Availability: The EA is available on DOE's National Energy Technology Laboratory (NETL) website at http://www.netl.doe.gov/publications/others/nepa/ea.html.

ACRONYMS AND ABBREVIATIONS

CFR   *Code of Federal Regulations*

CHP   combined heat and power

DOE   U.S. Department of Energy

EA   environmental assessment

EPA   U.S. Environmental Protection Agency

FR   *Federal Register*

FWS   U.S. Fish and Wildlife Service

NEPA   National Environmental Policy Act of 1969, as amended

NETL   National Energy Technology Laboratory

PM_{10} particulate matter with median aerodynamic diameter of 10 micrometers or less

$PM_{2.5}$ particulate matter with median aerodynamic diameter of 2.5 micrometers or less

Stat.   *United States Statutes at Large*

U.S.C.   *United States Code*

CONTENTS

LIST OF TABLES

LIST OF FIGURES

APPENDIXES

SUMMARY

The U.S. Department of Energy (DOE or the Department) proposes to award a $10 million financial assistance grant in a cost-sharing arrangement under the American Recovery and Reinvestment Act of 2009 (Recovery Act) to Texas A&M University (Texas A&M or the University). The grant would fund in part the proposed project, which is to install and operate a high-efficiency combined heat and power (CHP) system and supporting infrastructure on the University's campus in College Station, Texas. The cost of equipment installation and startup of the proposed project would be approximately $70.3 million.

At present, Texas A&M's Central Utility Plant uses two natural gas industrial boilers to produce steam for the generation of electricity, chilled water, hot water for heating, domestic hot water, and steam. The University buys the balance of its electricity from the local grid. The proposed project would install and operate a 34-megawatt natural gas combustion turbine, a 210,000-pound-per-hour heat recovery steam generator, and an 11-megawatt steam turbine generator. The system would produce steam for heating and cooling and to generate electricity. DOE evaluated commonly addressed environmental resource areas and identified no significant adverse impacts from the proposed project. DOE determined for some resource areas that there would be no impacts or the potential impacts would be small, temporary, or both and therefore did not carry those forward for additional analysis. DOE focused its analyses on those environmental resource areas that could require new or amended permits, have the potential for significant impacts or controversy, or typically interest the public, such as socioeconomics. DOE performed more detailed analyses of potential impacts for air quality, water resources, waste, and socioeconomics and environmental justice. The following paragraphs summarize the analyses.

Air Quality. Air emissions during construction for the proposed project on the College Station campus would include combustion emissions from vehicles and heavy-duty equipment and fugitive dust from site preparation activities. These emissions would have short-term adverse impacts that Texas A&M could mitigate through best management practices such as soil stabilization and watering of exposed soils. Fugitive dust emissions would cease on completion of construction, so long-term impacts would be negligible.

Operation of the proposed CHP system would increase some of the Central Utility Plant emissions (PM_{10}, sulfur dioxide, and volatile organic compounds). These emissions could be offset by reductions in emissions at other fossil-fuel electric plants because Texas A&M would purchase significantly less electricity from the regional grid. Emission of carbon monoxide would be lower, and emission of nitrogen oxides would be much lower. Texas A&M would install 45 megawatts of power-generating capacity and reduce the University's carbon dioxide emissions.

Water Resources. The College Station campus is in the Brazos River watershed. The river lies about eight miles west of campus. There are no surface water bodies at the Central Utility Plant or along the routes for electrical work. The closest water bodies are ponds on the campus golf course.

The proposed project would use groundwater from four local aquifers. During construction, Texas A&M would use appropriate erosion control and storm water management measures to reduce the impacts of erosion and increased runoff under its general construction storm water permit. During operations, the University would discharge wastewater after treatment to its current storm water system, which drains to the Brazos River through several tributaries. The main source of wastewater would be from boiler blowdown, which contains carbonates and scaling materials. The proposed project would have a small impact on the quantity of wastewater the University discharges, and there would be no change in the quality of that wastewater. The current Texas A&M industrial discharge permit would not require modification. Impacts to groundwater availability and quality would be unlikely from normal operations. The University would prevent or mitigate potential impacts from accidental spills of contaminants by following a spill prevention and mitigation plan.

None of the proposed construction activities would occur in a 100-year floodplain, and there are no wetlands in the proposed project areas, so there would be no impacts to floodplains and wetlands.

Waste. Construction for the proposed project would generate construction-related debris such as wood, metal, and concrete. Texas A&M would recycle some of this waste and ship the remainder to a permitted commercial landfill. During normal operations, Texas A&M would generate miscellaneous municipal wastes (for example, wood, paper, garbage, and absorbents) and a minor amount of hazardous waste (aqueous ammonia and metal catalyst) that would not affect regional landfills or treatment plants.

Socioeconomics and Environmental Justice. The proposed project would have the beneficial impact of creating new direct and indirect jobs during construction and operations and stimulating the economic base of the community. DOE expects that members of the community's existing labor force would fill the new jobs, so there would be no adverse impacts to the existing infrastructure or social services. In relation to environmental justice, there would be no adverse and disproportionate impacts to minority and low-income populations because there would be no high and adverse impacts to any member of the community.

Cumulative impact considerations included additional utilities work such as a new natural gas pipeline, College Station campus construction projects, the Research Valley Innovation Center, and projects at the Easterwood Airport. These projects would contribute cumulative short-term impacts to traffic but would also have beneficial socioeconomic impacts. In addition, DOE considered the rapid growth of the College Station-Bryan Metropolitan Statistical Area. The cumulative impacts of this growth would include the loss of vacant land and the need to expand utility services and infrastructure. In addition, expansion could put pressure on social services such as medical care, schools, and fire and police services.

In terms of the No-Action Alternative, DOE assumed Texas A&M would not proceed with the project without DOE assistance. Therefore, there would be no impacts to any resource category. However, the above-described potentials for positive impacts to air quality and socioeconomics would also not occur. In addition, DOE's ability to achieve its objectives under the Industrial Technologies Program and the Recovery Act would be impaired.

1. INTRODUCTION

As part of the American Recovery and Reinvestment Act of 2009 (the Recovery Act; Public Law 111-5, 123 Stat. 115), the U.S. Department of Energy (DOE or the Department) National Energy Technology Laboratory (NETL), on behalf of the Office of Energy Efficiency and Renewable Energy's Industrial Technologies Program, is providing up to $156 million in federal funding for competitively awarded grants for the deployment of projects for district energy systems, combined heat and power (CHP) systems, waste energy recovery systems, and energy-efficient industrial equipment and processes at single or multiple installations and sites. The funding of the selected projects requires compliance with the National Environmental Policy Act of 1969 (NEPA; 42 U.S.C. 4321 et seq.), Council on Environmental Quality regulations (40 CFR Parts 1500 to 1508), and DOE NEPA implementing procedures (10 CFR Part 1021).

To comply with NEPA, DOE prepared this *Final Environmental Assessment for the Texas A&M University Combined Heat and Power Project, College Station, Texas* (EA). This EA examines the potential environmental consequences of DOE's proposed action, providing financial assistance, and the Texas A&M University (Texas A&M or the University) proposed project, which is to install and operate a high-efficiency CHP system at its campus in College Station, Texas. College Station is in Brazos County. At present, Texas A&M's Central Utility Plant uses two natural gas industrial boilers to produce steam for the generation of electricity, chilled water production, hot water production for heating, domestic hot water production, and steam. The University buys the balance of its electricity from the local grid. The University is engaged in an expansion and upgrade of its electrical, heating, and cooling systems.

The proposed project would install and operate a 34-megawatt natural gas turbine generator, a 210,000-pound-per hour heat recovery steam generator, and an 11-megawatt steam turbine generator (Nelson 2010). In combination with existing equipment the University would keep, the upgraded system would produce steam for heating and cooling and provide up to 45 megawatts of power-generating capacity (Hightower 2010a). The proposed project would convert heat energy from the natural-gas-fired turbine to drive the generator and to produce waste heat for the heat recovery steam generator. The steam would drive steam turbine generators to produce electricity.

This chapter explains NEPA and related regulations (Section 1.1), the background of the Industrial Technologies Program (Section 1.2), the Department's purpose and need for action (Section 1.3), the environmental resources DOE did not carry forward to detailed analysis (Section 1.4), and the consultation and public comment process (Section 1.5). Chapter 2 discusses DOE's proposed action, Texas A&M's proposed project, the No-Action Alternative, and DOE's Alternative Actions. Chapter 3 details the affected environment and the potential environmental consequences of the proposed project and of the No-Action Alternative and considers resource commitments. Chapter 4 addresses cumulative impacts, and Chapter 5 provides DOE's conclusions from the analyses. Chapter 6 lists the references for this document. Appendix A contains the distribution list, and Appendix B contains correspondence between DOE, the Texas State Historic Preservation Officer, and the U.S. Fish and Wildlife Service (FWS).

1.1 National Environmental Policy Act and Related Regulations

In accordance with its NEPA implementing procedures, DOE must evaluate the potential environmental impacts of funding decisions. Therefore, this EA examines the potential direct, indirect, and cumulative environmental impacts of the proposed project and of the No-Action Alternative. The No-Action Alternative provides a basis of comparison between the proposed project's impacts and those that would occur if DOE did not provide funding to support the construction and operation of a CHP system on the College Station campus.

DOE must comply with the requirements of NEPA before it can make a final decision to proceed with a proposed federal action that could cause adverse impacts to human health or the environment. This EA fulfills DOE's obligations under NEPA and provides DOE with the information necessary to make an informed decision about the installation and operation of a CHP system that would produce steam for heating and cooling and generate electricity.

1.2 Background of the Industrial Technologies Program

DOE's National Energy Technology Laboratory manages the research and development portfolio of the Industrial Technologies Program for the Office of Energy Efficiency and Renewable Energy. The mission of the Industrial Technologies Program is to establish U.S. industry as a world leader in energy efficiency and productivity. The Program leads the national effort to reduce industrial energy intensity and carbon emissions, and strives to transform the way U.S. industry uses energy by supporting cost-shared research and development that addresses the top energy challenges facing industry. In addition, the Industrial Technologies Program fosters the adoption of advanced technologies and energy management best practices to produce meaningful progress in reducing industrial energy intensity.

Congress appropriated significant funding for the Industrial Technologies Program in the Recovery Act to stimulate the economy and reduce unemployment in addition to furthering the objectives of the existing Program. DOE solicited applications for this funding by issuing a competitive Funding Opportunity Announcement (DE-FOA-0000044), *Recovery Act: Deployment of Combined Heat and Power (CHP) Systems, District Energy Systems, Waste Energy Recovery Systems, and Efficient Industrial Equipment,* on July 7, 2009. The announcement invited applications in four areas of interest:

- Area of Interest 1 – Combined Heat and Power; the generation of electric energy and heat in a single, integrated system, with an overall thermal efficiency of 60 percent or greater on a higher-heating-value basis.

- Area of Interest 2 – District Energy Systems; systems providing thermal energy from a renewable energy source, thermal energy source, or highly efficient technology to more than one building or fixed energy-consuming use from one or more thermal energy production facilities through pipes or other means to provide space heating, space conditioning, hot water, steam, compression, process energy, or other end uses.

- Area of Interest 3 – Industrial Waste Energy Recovery; the collection and reuse of energy from sources such as exhaust heat or flared gas from any industrial process; waste gas or industrial tail gas that would otherwise be flared, incinerated, or vented; a pressure drop in any gas, excluding any pressure drop to a condenser that subsequently vents the resulting heat.

- Area of Interest 4 – Efficient Industrial Equipment; any proven commercially available technology that can provide a minimum 25-percent efficiency improvement into the industrial sector.

DOE announced its selections on November 3, 2009, with multiple awards in three of the four areas of interest. DOE selected nine projects based on the evaluation criteria in the funding opportunity announcement and gave special consideration to projects that promoted the objectives of the Recovery Act—job preservation or creation and economic recovery—in an expeditious manner.

The proposed project covered in this EA, installation and start-up of a CHP system on the Texas A&M College Station campus, was one of the nine projects DOE selected for funding. DOE's proposed action would provide $10 million in financial assistance under a cost-sharing arrangement with Texas A&M. The cost of the University's overall plan would be about $70.3 million (Riley 2010).

1.3 Purpose and Need for DOE Action

The purpose of the proposed action is to support the mission of DOE's Industrial Technologies Program and the goals of the Recovery Act. The mission of the Industrial Technologies Program is to have U.S. industry lead the world in energy efficiency and productivity. The Program leads the national effort to reduce industrial energy intensity and carbon emissions, and strives to transform the way U.S. industry uses energy by supporting cost-shared research and development that addresses the top energy challenges facing industry. In addition, the Program fosters the adoption of today's advanced technologies and energy management best practices to produce meaningful progress in reducing industrial energy intensity.

The Industrial Technologies Program's three-part strategy pursues this mission by:

- Sponsoring research, development, and demonstration of industry-specific and crosscutting technologies to reduce energy and carbon intensity;

- Conducting technology delivery activities to help plants access today's technology and management practices; and

- Promoting a corporate culture of energy efficiency and carbon management within industry.

To align with its mission, the program established a goal of achieving a 25-percent reduction in industrial energy intensity by 2017, guided by the *Energy Policy Act of 2005*. The strategy also calls for an 18-percent reduction in U.S. carbon intensity by 2012. The Department seeks to identify projects and technologies that it can fund to meet this goal.

In June 2009, DOE initiated a process to identify suitable projects by issuing Funding Opportunity Announcement DE-FOA-00000044, *Recovery Act: Deployment of Combined Heat and Power (CHP) Systems, District Energy Systems, Waste Energy Recovery Systems, and Efficient Industrial Equipment*. This Funding Opportunity Announcement is funded by the Recovery Act.

The Recovery Act seeks to create jobs, restore economic growth, and strengthen America's middle class through measures that modernize the nation's infrastructure, enhance America's energy independence, expand educational opportunities, preserve and improve affordable health care, provide tax relief, and protect those in greatest need. Provision of funds under this Funding Opportunity Announcement would achieve these objectives.

The capital cost of new equipment is often a roadblock for use of more efficient equipment and processes. Although the newer technologies would provide lower energy requirements and operating costs, the payback period for some technologies does not meet internal business goals. DOE's provision of financial assistance allows companies to reduce the payback period, making these new technologies an acceptable option for them.

1.4 Environmental Resources Not Carried Forward

Chapter 3 of this EA describes the affected environment and examines the potential environmental impacts of the proposed project and the No-Action Alternative for the following resource areas:

- Air quality,
- Water resources,
- Waste, and
- Socioeconomics and environmental justice.

The focus of the more detailed analyses in Chapter 3 is on those resources that could require new or amended permits, have the potential for significant impacts or controversy, or typically interest the public, such as socioeconomics.

DOE EAs also commonly address the environmental resource areas listed in Table 1-1. However, in an effort to streamline the NEPA process and enable a timely award to the selected project, DOE did not examine the resource areas in the table at the same level of detail as the above-mentioned four areas. Table 1-1 describes the Department's evaluation of these resource areas. In each case, there would be no impacts or the potential impacts would be small or temporary in nature, or both. Therefore, DOE determined that further analysis is unnecessary.

In terms of the No-Action Alternative, the impacts Table 1-1 lists would not occur because DOE assumes the proposed project would not proceed.

Table 1-1. Environmental resource areas with no, small, or temporary impacts.

Environmental resource area	Impact consideration and conclusions
Geology and soils	The proposed project area consists mainly of the Central Utility Plant, which has been industrialized since the 1890s. There is no record of site stability issues. The portions of the site that do not host existing structures have at some point been previously disturbed. The University is also installing underground concrete-enclosed electrical ducts by trenching along existing roadways and across the drill field. During construction, Texas A&M would use best management practices to control potential surface runoff and soil erosion.
Land use	The proposed project site's current land use is industrial; it provides the campus with steam and electricity. The land use of the site would not change under the proposed project. The plant is within the boundary of the Texas A&M campus and would not generate changes in land uses near the University.
Aesthetics and visual resources	The proposed project area has no aesthetic or visual resources of interest. The proposed project would not alter the existing visual characteristics from within or near the site.
Noise	The noise level of the new equipment is expected be less than 85 A-weighted decibels at 3 feet. The noise would appreciably reduce as distance from the equipment increased. DOE does not expect noise levels outside the Central Utility Plant to be much greater than current ambient noise levels.
Biological resources	DOE reviewed the FWS list of federally threatened, endangered, and candidate species for Brazos County, Texas. There are two endangered species and two candidate species. The endangered species are the Navasona ladies'-tresses (*Spiranthes parksii*) and the whooping crane (*Grus Americana*). The two candidate species are both fish, the sharpnose Shiner (*Notropis oxyrthynchus*) and the smalleye Shiner (*Notropis buccula*) (FWS 2010). The potential impacts of the proposed project would be primarily limited to the previously disturbed and industrialized Central Utility Plant. DOE has reviewed the habitat and foraging requirements of the above species and determined that there would be no effect on federally listed threatened, endangered, or candidate species. Appendix B contains a copy of a letter from DOE to the FWS consistent with Section 7 review requirements under the Endangered Species Act of 1973, as amended (16 U.S.C. 1531 et seq.).

Table 1-1. Environmental resource areas with no, small, or temporary impacts (continued).

Environmental resource area	Impact consideration and conclusions
Occupational health and safety	Texas A&M maintains a comprehensive health and safety management system for its employees to control exposure to workplace hazards and injury. The University's occupational health and safety system includes a program for injury reduction, formal accident investigation procedures, and facility inspections (TAMU 2010). The University also maintains a safety hotline and complies with the reporting requirements of the State of Texas. Incident rates among workers on the utilities mission at Texas A&M have been below the state average for similar types of work. Employee growth to operate facilities under the proposed project would be minimal, and DOE expects incident rates to remain consistent with the University's historical rates. In relation to the short-term construction period, DOE expects the incident rates would be consistent with those for nonresidential building construction jobs. The total recordable cases incidence rate in 2008 for nonresidential building construction jobs was 4.4 injuries per 100 full-time employees, and the incidence rate for days away from work, days of restricted work activity, or job transfer was 2.2 injuries per 100 full-time employees (BLS 2009).
Historic and cultural resources	There are no known federally listed or eligible historic sites within or near the project site. Several buildings in the Central Utility Plant are more than 45 years old but have no historical or architectural interest. DOE has determined there would be no effects on federally listed or candidate historic sites. Appendix B contains a letter from DOE to the Texas State Historic Preservation Officer in relation to formal consultation pursuant to Section 106 of the National Historic Preservation Act, as amended (16 U.S.C. 470 et seq.), and the provisions of 36 CFR Part 800. The State Historic Preservation Officer concurred with DOE's determination by returning the Department's letter stamped, "No Historic Properties Affected, Project May Proceed" (Appendix B).
Utilities, energy, and materials	Under the proposed project, there would be a positive benefit to the campus utility infrastructure. The installation of a high-efficiency CHP system would reduce reliance on commercially purchased electricity and further reduce the University's carbon footprint. Part of the project is the installation of 2 miles of electrical ductwork and the upgrade of four switching stations. The project would require concrete, wood, and steel for construction and fuel and oil for construction vehicles. Operations would require about 3 trillion British thermal units of natural gas per year.
Transportation	The University manages an existing on-campus roadway system, parking facilities, and bus routes. During the construction phase for the proposed action, including the installation of underground electrical ducts, some roads and parking facilities would be temporarily closed. The University operates a program to disseminate information about road and parking lot closures to its students, faculty, and staff.

1.5 Consultations and Public Comment Response Process

DOE issued the Draft EA for comment on August 8, 2010, and advertised its release in *The Eagle* on August 8, 9, and 10. In addition, the Department sent a copy for public review to the

Larry J. Ringer (College Station) public library. The Department established a 15-day public comment period that began August 8, 2010, and ended August 22, 2010, and announced it would accept comments by mail, email, or facsimile. Before the release of the EA for public comment, DOE sent project information to the Texas State Historic Preservation Officer and the FWS for their consideration.

1.5.1 CONSULTATIONS

Texas State Historic Preservation Officer

On July 1, 2010, DOE sent a formal consultation letter to the Texas State Historic Preservation Officer in accordance with the review requirements of Section 106 of the National Historic Preservation Act, as amended (16 U.S.C. 470 et seq.), and implementing regulations at 36 CFR Part 800. The letter detailed DOE's investigation of nearby historic properties and concluded that no historic properties would be affected by the proposed project.

The Texas State Historic Preservation Officer responded on July 16, 2010, and concurred with DOE's finding. Appendix B contains copies of both letters.

U.S. Fish and Wildlife Service

On July 12, 2010, DOE sent an informational letter to the FWS and a copy of the Draft EA. The FWS had no comments on the Draft EA.

1.5.2 COMMENT-RESPONSE PROCESS

DOE received no comments on the Draft EA.

2. DOE PROPOSED ACTION AND ALTERNATIVES

This chapter describes DOE's proposed action (Section 2.1); Texas A&M's proposed project (Section 2.2), the No-Action Alternative (Section 2.3), and DOE Alternative Actions (Section 2.4).

2.1 DOE's Proposed Action

DOE's proposed action is to provide a financial assistance grant to facilitate the installation of a CHP system that would provide heat and cooling and generate electricity. DOE would award a Recovery Act grant of $10 million in a cost-sharing arrangement with Texas A&M, which estimates the cost of its overall plan to be about $70.3 million (Riley 2010).

2.2 Texas A&M's Proposed Project

Texas A&M's proposed project would install and operate a high-efficiency CHP system that would generate steam for heating and cooling as well as electricity. Texas A&M would install the CHP system at its College Station campus in Brazos County, Texas, about 80 miles northeast of Austin. The campus occupies 8,000 acres and serves over 46,000 undergraduate and 8,500 graduate students. The University has been in operation since 1876 and is the largest employer in College Station (TAMU 2009). Figure 2-1 provides a map showing the approximate location of College Station.

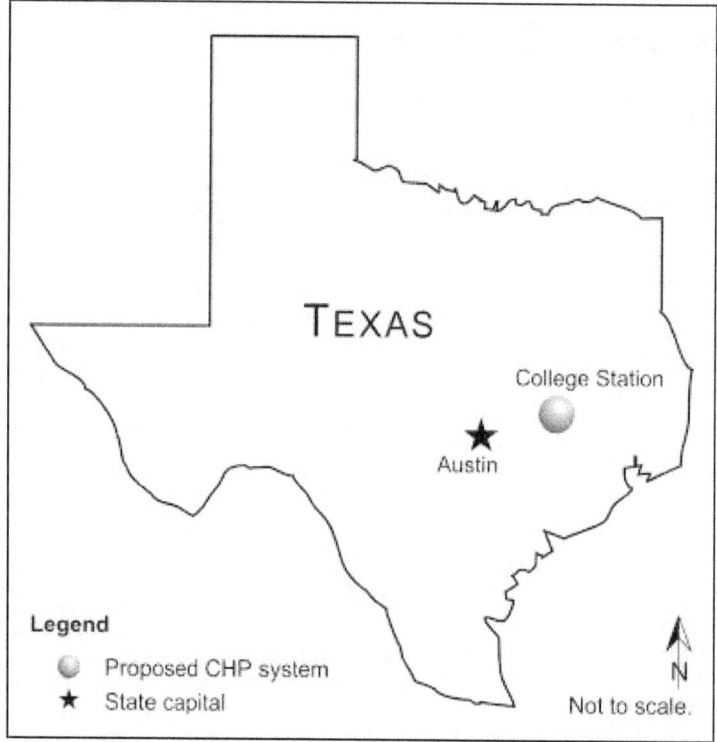

Figure 2-1. General location of College Station.

The University is expanding, and the proposed project this EA describes is part of a larger plan to upgrade the Central Utility Plant and campus electrical distribution system to serve that expansion. Texas A&M has been self-generating electrical power and steam since 1893 at its Central Utility Plant at 493 Ireland Street (Figure 2-2). CHP generation equipment has a typical useful life of 30 years. The equipment that would be replaced, under this proposed project, was installed in 1971. In recent years, the University has been purchasing increasing amounts of electricity from the grid because the older equipment lacks sufficient efficiency.

Figure 2-2. Satellite view of the College Station campus showing the location of the Central Utility Plant.

The proposed project would primarily occur within the boundaries of the existing Central Utility Plant on the campus, which consists of several buildings and support structures. In addition, Texas A&M would install about 2 miles of underground concrete-encased electrical duct and upgrade four switching stations. The installation of the ducts would involve trenching along existing roadways and across the drill field. Figure 2-3 shows the approximate routes for the ducts and locations of the switching stations.

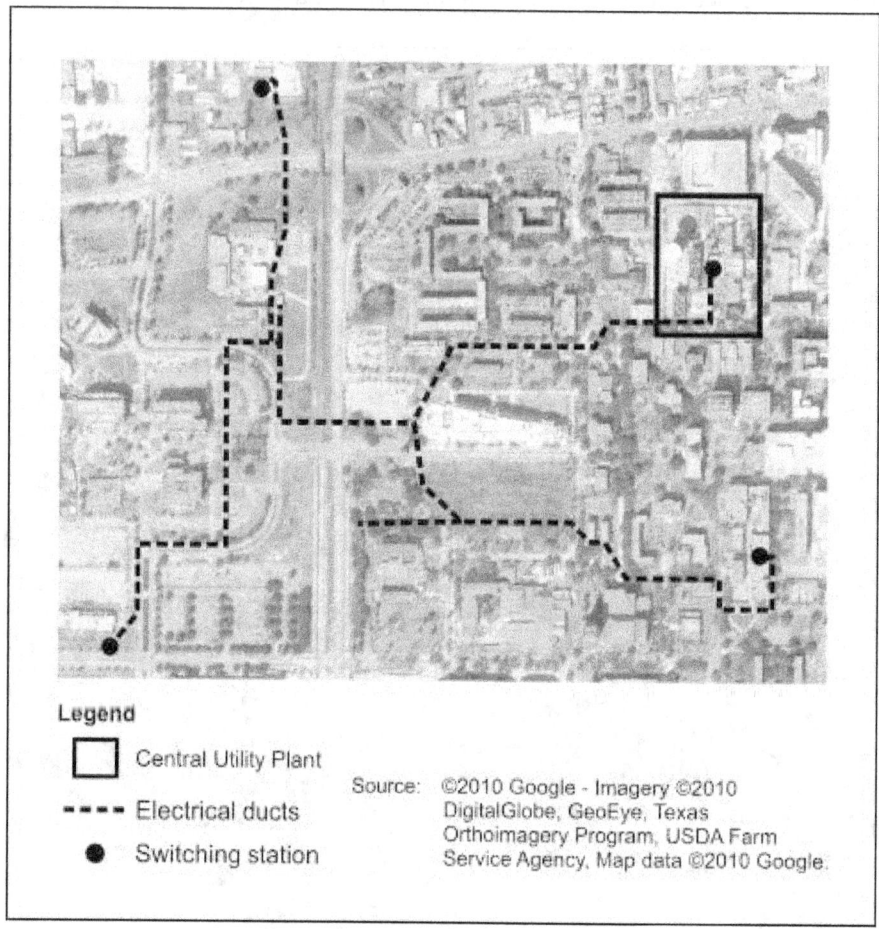

Legend

☐ Central Utility Plant

- - - - Electrical ducts

● Switching station

Source: ©2010 Google - Imagery ©2010 DigitalGlobe, GeoEye, Texas Orthoimagery Program, USDA Farm Service Agency, Map data ©2010 Google.

Figure 2-3. Approximate routes of electrical ducts and locations of switching stations.

The proposed project would require construction of foundations and enclosures for a 34-megawatt natural gas combustion turbine and a 210,000-pound-per-hour heat recovery steam generator. The University would install an 11-megawatt steam turbine generator in an existing building. The project would include associated operating equipment and piping between new and existing Central Utility Plant equipment (Riley 2010). The proposed project would convert heat energy from the natural-gas-fired turbine to drive the generator and to produce waste heat for the heat recovery steam generator. The steam would drive steam turbine generators to produce electricity. Figure 2-4 provides a schematic of the CHP system (Hightower 2010a).

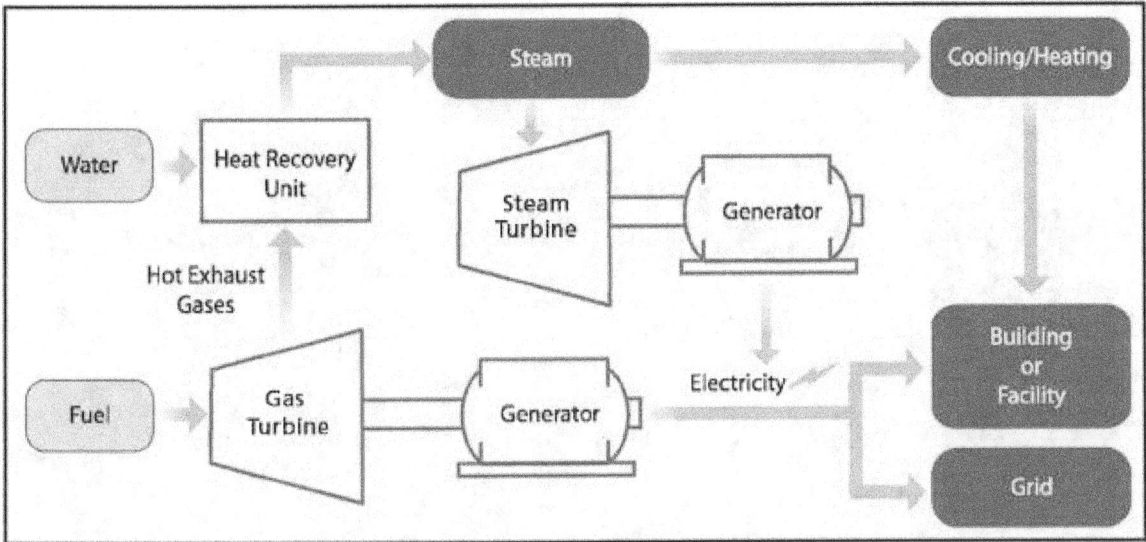

Figure 2-4. Schematic showing the CHP system.

Installation and startup of the CHP system along with the electrical upgrades, which is the proposed project in this EA, would take about 26 months (Riley 2009). Major project elements include the following (Figure 2-5):

- Constructing a new foundation and structure to house the new 34-megawatt gas turbine generator and auxiliary equipment,

- Constructing a new foundation and structure to support the new heat recovery steam generator, and

- Modifying an existing building to house the new 11-megawatt steam turbine generator.

In addition, Texas A&M would upgrade an existing boiler and retire two steam turbine generators, one gas turbine generator, one boiler, and one heat recovery steam generator.

In combination with existing equipment the University would keep, the system would produce up to 710,000 pounds per hour of steam for heating and cooling (including standby capacity) (Nelson 2010) and provide up to 45 megawatts of power-generating capacity (Hightower 2010a). The system would provide up to two-thirds of the University's electricity needs and a significant percentage of the campus heating and cooling requirements, thereby substantially improving the overall efficiency, reliability, and emissions profile of the campus Central Utility Plant. The proposed CHP system would have an expected lifetime of 30 years.

Specific and measurable energy savings of Texas A&M's project would include (TAMU 2009):

- Energy savings of over 1 trillion British thermal units per year,

Figure 2-5. Aerial photograph of site preparation underway showing locations of major new equipment.

- Energy cost savings of $6 to $9 million per year,

- Reduction in campus carbon dioxide emissions of 143,000 tons (about 29 percent) per year, and

- Reduction, over the life of the system, of 10 million megawatt-hours for electricity the University would require from the regional electrical grid.

Once in operation, Texas A&M would closely monitor the CHP system performance and report to DOE and other agencies to foster understanding of the benefits of CHP technology. The electricity the University would no longer buy from the grid would become available for other applications and potentially delay the need for new fossil-fuel plant construction in the region.

2.3 No-Action Alternative

Under the No-Action Alternative, DOE would not provide financial assistance for the proposed project. As a result, the project would be delayed as Texas A&M sought other funding sources to meet its needs or abandoned if other funding sources could not be obtained. As a result,

DOE's ability to achieve its objectives under the Industrial Technologies Program and the Recovery Act would be impaired.

Although this and other selected projects might proceed if DOE decided not to provide financial assistance, the Department assumes for purposes of this environmental analysis that the project would not proceed without its assistance. If Texas A&M did proceed without DOE's financial assistance, the potential impacts would be essentially identical to those if the Department provided the funding. To allow a comparison between the potential impacts of a project as implemented and the impacts of not proceeding with a project, DOE assumes that, if it were to decide to withhold assistance from a project, the project would not proceed.

2.4 DOE Alternative Actions

DOE's alternatives to this project consist of the nine technically acceptable applications it received in response to the Funding Opportunity Announcement, "Recovery Act: Deployment of Combined Heat and Power (CHP) Systems, District Energy Systems, Waste Energy Recovery Systems, and Efficient Industrial Equipment" (DE-FOA-0000044). Before selection, DOE made preliminary determinations about the level of review under NEPA based on potentially significant impacts identified during review of the technically acceptable applications. DOE conducted these preliminary reviews pursuant to 10 CFR 1021.216 and a variance to certain requirements in the regulation granted by the Department's General Counsel (74 FR 41963; August 18, 2009). These preliminary NEPA determinations and reviews were provided to the selection official for consideration during the selection process.

Because DOE's proposed action is limited to providing financial assistance in cost-sharing arrangements to selected applicants in response to a competitive funding opportunity, DOE's decision is limited to either accepting or rejecting the project as proposed by the proponent, including its proposed technology and selected sites. DOE's consideration of reasonable alternatives is therefore limited to the technically acceptable applications and the No-Action Alternative for each selected project.

3. AFFECTED ENVIRONMENT AND ENVIRONMENTAL CONSEQUENCES

Sections 3.1 to 3.4 detail the affected environment and potential environmental consequences for the proposed project and the No-Action Alternative. The sections discuss air quality, water resources, waste, and socioeconomics and environmental justice, respectively. Section 3.5 discusses resource commitments.

3.1 Air Quality

Section 3.1.1 discusses regional air quality and provides 2009 baseline conditions, and Section 3.1.2 provides a comparison of existing emissions with those for Texas A&M's proposed project.

3.1.1 AFFECTED ENVIRONMENT

The ambient air quality in an area can be characterized in terms of whether it complies with the primary and secondary National Ambient Air Quality Standards. The Clean Air Act (42 U.S.C. 7401 et seq.) requires the U.S. Environmental Protection Agency (EPA) to set national standards for pollutants that are considered harmful to public health and the environment. The EPA established standards for six criteria pollutants: carbon monoxide, lead, nitrogen dioxide, ozone, particulate matter [with median aerodynamic diameters of less than or equal to 10 micrometers (PM_{10}) and less than or equal to 2.5 micrometers ($PM_{2.5}$)], and sulfur dioxide. Primary standards define levels of air quality for each of the six criteria pollutants that would provide an adequate margin of safety to protect public health including the health of sensitive populations such as children and the elderly. Secondary standards define levels of air quality that are deemed necessary to protect the public welfare including protection against decreased visibility and damage to animals, crops, vegetation, and buildings.

Texas A&M operates a Central Utility Plant at its campus in College Station, Brazos County, Texas. The EPA has designated Brazos County as in attainment of the National Ambient Air Quality Standards. In recent years, the Central Utility Plant has operated with two boilers and one gas turbine generator. The University holds multiple New Source Review permits and a Title V permit. The gas turbine generator is in the process of being removed from the Central Utility Plant. Table 3-1 lists 2009 emissions for Texas A&M's Central Utility Plant, which includes emissions from the gas turbine generator.

3.1.2 ENVIRONMENTAL CONSEQUENCES

3.1.2.1 Proposed Project

3.1.2.1.1 Construction Impacts

Air emissions from construction activities for Texas A&M's proposed project would include combustion emissions from vehicles and heavy-duty equipment the University would use during

Table 3-1. 2009 Texas A&M air emissions.

Pollutant	Total emissions (tons per year)
PM_{10}	4.9
Nitrogen oxides	115
Carbon monoxide	31
Sulfur dioxide	2.8
Volatile organic compounds	2.8

Source: Hightower 2010b.

construction of new facilities and fugitive dust from site preparation activities. These emissions would have short-term adverse impacts that Texas A&M could mitigate through best management practices such as soil stabilization and watering of exposed soils. Fugitive dust emissions would end on completion of construction, so long-term impacts would be negligible.

3.1.2.1.2 *Operations Impacts*

The proposed project consists of a 34-megawatt natural gas combustion turbine, a 210,000-pound-per-hour heat recovery steam generator, an 11-megawatt steam turbine (Table 3-2) (Nelson 2010). This new equipment, together with one older steam turbine generator that would remain in service, would provide a total of 45 megawatts of self-generation power capacity at Texas A&M (Hightower 2010a).

Table 3-2. Proposed new and existing equipment.

Equipment	Capacity
Proposed gas turbine generator	34 megawatts
Proposed steam turbine generator	11 megawatts
Existing steam turbine generator	5 megawatts
Proposed heat recovery steam generator	210,000 pounds per hour
Existing boiler	300,000 pounds per hour
Existing boiler	200,000 pounds per hour

The new CHP system would have an overall efficiency above 75 percent, and would use 3 trillion British thermal units of natural gas per year (Riley 2009). The University would keep the existing boilers on standby but would operate them only when the gas turbine needed maintenance activities or other shutdown events.

Table 3-3 lists current emissions estimates from existing power generation at Texas A&M, estimated emissions from the proposed project (as provided in the air permit; Inman 2010), estimated reductions in emissions from the removal of the existing gas turbine, and the total estimated emissions during routine operations under the proposed project. Texas A&M's proposed emissions control technologies would include a selective catalytic reduction unit that would remove about 90 percent of the nitrogen oxides from the new gas turbine exhaust. In combination with retiring the existing gas turbine, the proposed project would reduce nitrogen oxide emissions by about 78 tons per year.

Table 3-3. Existing Texas A&M emissions and proposed project emissions estimates (tons per year).

Pollutant	2009 Texas A&M emissions	Project's permitted emission levels	Reductions in emissions from removal of existing gas turbine	Total projected emissions
PM_{10}	4.9	4	1.8	7.1
Nitrogen oxides	115	10	88	37
Carbon monoxide	31	6.3	23	14.3
Sulfur dioxide	2.8	6	2.6	6.2
Volatile organic compounds	2.8	11	0.58	13.2

Source: Hightower 2010a,b; Inman 2010.
Note: Values generated using EPA AP-42 emission factors.
PM_{10} = particulate matter with median aerodynamic diameter of 10 micrometers or less.

The Clean Air Act requires that major air pollution sources undergoing construction or modification comply with all applicable Prevention of Significant Deterioration provisions (40 CFR 52.21) and nonattainment area New Source Review requirements. The Prevention of Significant Deterioration and nonattainment area New Source Review rules require certain analyses before a facility can obtain a permit to begin construction. Texas A&M would comply with any applicable emissions limits. The Prevention of Significant Deterioration provisions apply to new major sources or major modifications at existing sources for pollutants in attainment areas for a criteria pollutant. The Prevention of Significant Deterioration regulations require the use of the best available control technology to minimize emissions of pollutants. New Source Review, also referred to as construction permitting or preconstruction permitting, requires companies to obtain permits for new stationary sources of air pollution before beginning construction. Texas A&M has obtained an emissions permit from the Texas Commission on Environmental Quality to begin construction and would comply with any applicable emissions limits (Inman 2010).

Section 176(c)(1) of the Clean Air Act requires federal agencies to ensure that their actions conform to applicable implementation plans for the achievement and maintenance of the National Ambient Air Quality Standards for criteria pollutants (DOE 2000). To achieve conformity, a federal action must not contribute to new violations of standards for ambient air quality, increase the frequency or severity of existing violations, or delay timely attainment of standards in the area of concern. The EPA general conformity regulations (40 CFR Part 93, Subpart B) contain guidance for determining if a proposed federal action would cause emissions to be above specified levels in nonattainment or maintenance areas.

The Texas A&M CHP system would operate as an emissions source in accordance with State of Texas regulations for individual point source emissions. The proposed project would not exceed the threshold emission rate for criteria pollutants and would not represent 10 percent or more of the area's emissions inventory for those pollutants. Therefore, no conformity determination under the Clean Air Act would be necessary (DOE 2000).

Greenhouse Gas Emissions

The burning of fossil fuels, such as natural gas, emits carbon dioxide, which is a greenhouse gas. Greenhouse gases can trap heat in the atmosphere and have been associated with global climate change. The Intergovernmental Panel on Climate Change, in *Climate Change 2007: Synthesis Report, Summary for Policy Makers*, stated that warming of the earth's climate system is unequivocal, and that most of the observed increase in globally averaged temperatures since the mid-20th century is very likely due to the observed increase in concentrations of greenhouse gases from human activities (IPCC 2007). Greenhouse gases are well mixed throughout the lower atmosphere, such that any emissions would add to cumulative regional and global concentrations of carbon dioxide.

Because the proposed project would displace energy currently being supplied from the grid and would replace an aging power plant at the university, there would be a 140,000-ton reduction in regional greenhouse gas emissions and, therefore, no cumulative carbon impacts.

3.1.2.2 No-Action Alternative

Under the No-Action Alternative, there would be no increase in emissions of pollutants from the plant. However, there would be no beneficial decrease in regional emissions of pollutants from the use of the energy-efficient power generation plant.

3.2 Water Resources

Section 3.2.1 describes current conditions for groundwater, surface water, and wetlands; these form a basis of comparison for the impacts of Texas A&M's project in Section 3.2.2.

3.2.1 AFFECTED ENVIRONMENT

3.2.1.1 Surface Water

Texas A&M is in the Brazos River watershed. The Brazos River is about 8 miles west of campus. There are no surface water bodies on the proposed project site. The closest water bodies are ponds on the campus golf course.

Texas A&M discharges an average of 220,000 gallons of wastewater a day, with peak discharge in 2009 of 1.68 million gallons per day. The University has a current industrial discharge permit from the Texas Commission on Environmental Quality that covers the project site. The discharge path is via storm water piping to an unnamed waterway across the campus, which flows to Wolf Pen Creek, to Carter Creek, and then to the Brazos River (Hightower 2010c).

3.2.1.2 Groundwater

Texas A&M relies entirely on groundwater for its drinking water supply. The University pumps water from seven wells in four different aquifers: Sparta, Queen City, Carrizo, and Carrizo-

Wilcox. Texas A&M currently uses about 4.4 million gallons of water a day; the Central Utility Plant uses about 2.2 million gallons of water per day (Hightower 2010c).

The existing Central Utility Plant includes both aboveground and underground tanks to store products necessary to run the facility. The aboveground tanks store oil, acids, and other products. These tank systems include secondary containment to reduce air and water impacts from potential leaks or spills. The underground tanks store fuel oil.

3.2.1.3 Floodplains and Wetlands

The project location is not in a Federal Emergency Management Agency-designated 100-year floodplain. The proposed project location is the site of the existing energy facility. No wetlands are present at that location.

3.2.2 ENVIRONMENTAL CONSEQUENCES

3.2.2.1 Proposed Project

3.2.2.1.1 *Construction Impacts*

The two primary water resource concerns in relation to new construction at Texas A&M would be soil erosion and storm water runoff. Ground-disturbing activities would include demolition of existing foundations and construction of new buildings and structures with impermeable surfaces. Because exposed soils are subject to erosion, increased runoff could carry sediment into local waterways during precipitation events. Increased sedimentation in culverts, drainage systems, and waterways could impede surface water drainage from the site and increase the risk of flooding. However, Texas A&M would use appropriate erosion control and storm water management measures to reduce the impacts of erosion and increased runoff under its general construction storm water permit.

3.2.2.1.2 *Operations Impacts*

Surface Water

Texas A&M would not use surface water as a source of process water. The proposed project would discharge an additional 30,000 gallons a day to the Brazos River (McAnally 2010), which would increase the University's wastewater totals by less than 10 percent.

Groundwater

Water use at Texas A&M would increase minimally by about 58,000 gallons a day under the proposed project (McAnally 2010), which would be a 2-percent increase. The rate of withdrawals from the aquifers would be approximately the same as current operations. DOE does not expect impacts to the availability of groundwater.

Texas A&M would not require new underground storage tanks for the proposed project. The University would follow a spill prevention and mitigation plan to prevent or mitigate the potential for and effects from accidental spills of contaminants under 40 CFR Part 112. Where appropriate, aboveground storage tanks would include secondary containment systems that would be designed to contain spills or releases to minimize potential impacts.

Floodplains and Wetlands

None of the proposed construction activities would occur in a 100-year floodplain, and there are no wetlands in the area of construction. Therefore, there would be no impacts on floodplains or wetlands from construction or operation of the proposed project.

3.2.2.2   No-Action Alternative

Under the No-Action Alternative, water use and wastewater generation would not increase. Therefore, there would be no impacts to surface water, groundwater, floodplains, or wetlands.

3.3 Waste

Section 3.3.1 provides waste generation estimates for current Texas A&M operations as a basis of comparison for the estimated amounts of waste the University would generate under the proposed project (Section 3.3.2).

3.3.1 AFFECTED ENVIRONMENT

The existing Central Utility Plant includes both aboveground and underground tanks to store products necessary to run the facility. The aboveground tanks store oil, acids, and other products. These tank systems include secondary containment to reduce air and water impacts from potential leaks or spills. The underground storage tanks store fuel oil. Texas A&M does not store wastes that are subject to the Resource Conservation and Recovery Act of 1986, as amended (42 U.S.C. 6901 et seq.) in the underground storage tanks. The Central Utility Plant generates about 60 tons per year of municipal waste.

The primary, nonmunicipal waste stream is used lubricating oil and incidentals including filters and absorbents. The University disposed of about 8,700 pounds of used refrigeration oil in 2009. Other wastes that can be generated include solvents and paint waste, of which there were none in 2009.

3.3.2 ENVIRONMENTAL CONSEQUENCES

3.3.2.1 Proposed Project

3.3.2.1.1 *Construction Impacts*

Construction of the new Texas A&M power facilities would generate about 4,500 cubic yards of construction-related debris such as wood, metal, and concrete. The University would ship construction waste to the Brazos Valley Solid Waste Management Agency. The amount of construction waste would not be large enough to affect the existing capacity of the landfill. The University would recycle about 1,600 cubic yards of metal (Hightower 2010c).

3.3.2.1.2 *Operations Impacts*

The characteristics of the waste from operation of the proposed project would be similar to those Texas A&M currently generates. Under the proposed project, The University would use several hazardous chemicals on a regular basis including the following (Hightower 2010c):

- About 320 gallons per day of aqueous ammonia (about 19 percent ammonia and 81 percent water), which would be stored in an aboveground storage tank.

- About 480 cubic feet every 3 years of metal catalyst for the selective catalytic reduction unit.

Although the amounts of hazardous waste from the project would be very small and the CHP plant would likely qualify as a conditionally exempt small-quantity generator, Texas A&M would ship all hazardous waste to one or more treatment, storage, or disposal facilities under the Resource Conservation and Recovery Act.

3.3.2.2 No-Action Alternative

Under the No-Action Alternative, waste levels from proposed operations would remain about the same as those of current operations.

3.4 Socioeconomics and Environmental Justice

Section 3.4.1 describes the socioeconomic environment in Brazos County and Section 3.4.2 discusses the potential impacts in the county. Section 3.4.3 addresses environmental justice consequences in Brazos County.

3.4.1 AFFECTED ENVIRONMENT

The proposed project site is on the campus of Texas A&M University in College Station, Texas. College Station is in Brazos County and is part of the Bureau of the Census College Station-Bryan Texas Metropolitan Statistical Area (Metro Code 17780). Brazos County's estimated population of about 180,000 persons in 2009 reflects an 18.1-percent growth since 2000 (Bureau of the Census 2010a). The Metropolitan Statistical Area had a 2009 estimated population of about 212,000 (Bureau of the Census 2010b). In 2008, the Brazos County population was 83.1-percent white, 10.7-percent black, 4.5-percent Asian, and 0.4-percent American Indian or Alaskan Native. About 1.2 percent of the population reported themselves as being of two or more races. Persons of Hispanic or Latino origin made up 21 percent of the population (Bureau of the Census 2010a).

The county's employment figures reflect the urban nature of the community; the county hosted about 105,000 nonfarming jobs in 2008, of which about 32,000 jobs (30 percent) were in government and government enterprise. Virtually all of the jobs in this sector were at Texas A&M. An additional 11,000 jobs were in retail trade (11 percent) and about 10,000 (9 percent) were in health care and social assistance. Accommodations and food services and the professional, scientific, and technical services sectors were also major employment industries (BEA 2010a). Brazos County residents held about 87 percent of the total jobs in the county. People who lived in Burleson County to the southwest and Robertson County to the northwest, also part of the Metropolitan Statistical Area, held about 3 percent of the jobs. People who lived outside those counties held the remainder (Bureau of the Census 2003). The county's March 2010 labor force had an unemployment rate of 5.6 percent, which was less than the state's unemployment rate of 8.2 percent that month (BLS 2010).

The 2008 per capita income in Brazos County of about $27,500 was about 72 percent of the Texas per capita income (BEA 2010b). In 2008, about 25 percent of county residents and 16 percent of Texas residents were living in poverty (Bureau of the Census 2010a). Section 3.4.3 discusses racial minority and ethnic minority populations and the low-income population in more detail in relation to environmental justice.

3.4.2 ENVIRONMENTAL CONSEQUENCES

The proposed natural-gas-fired CHP system project would create direct jobs during construction and several jobs during operations. The new construction jobs would create indirect jobs via the multiplier effect, in which the wages workers spend create the need for additional jobs. Direct and indirect jobs include professional, skilled, and unskilled positions; they would occur among suppliers of goods and services, including the university, and for the vendors of materials those suppliers would use to fashion goods and services. Earnings from this $70.3 million project in these direct and indirect jobs would generate wages and income that local, state, and federal governments would tax. In addition, these wages would lead to an increase in banking deposits, which would increase the regional lending base, and to spending on consumable and durable goods and services. The increase in jobs and wages in the community would have a small, positive impact.

The region's construction labor pool and the large employment base in the professional, scientific, and technical services sector and in the construction sector are adequate to support the labor demands of the project. DOE expects that all workers in new positions would be part of the existing labor force in the College Station-Bryan Texas Metropolitan Statistical Area, primarily in Brazos County. The additional jobs would be unlikely to cause a noticeable increase in the local population from workers moving into the area. Therefore, impacts to the existing infrastructure, housing, medical care, social services, police and fire protection, schools, or other community services would be unlikely, and DOE does not address these resources further.

3.4.2.1 Proposed Project

3.4.2.1.1 *Construction Impacts*

Preoperational activities, including design and engineering tasks, procurement of materials, construction of facilities, installation of equipment, and project startup at Texas A&M would take about 26 months (Riley 2009). These preoperational activities would create about 290 direct jobs, which would create about 310 additional indirect jobs; therefore, the Brazos County area would have about 600 new jobs (290 direct and 310 indirect) during the preoperational period (TAMU 2009). The 600 jobs would represent about 0.6 percent of the nonfarm employment in Brazos County in 2008 (BEA 2010a). Table 3-4 summarizes this information.

Table 3-4. New direct and indirect jobs during construction.[a]

Job type	Number of jobs
Direct	290
Indirect	310
Total	600

Source: TAMU 2009.

a. Includes jobs created by total project expenditures, including federal and nonfederal dollars.

The aggregate number of jobs would have a small, positive impact on the labor force by creating job opportunities that could reduce unemployment and increase labor participation. DOE expects that residents of Brazos County specifically, and residents of the College Station-Bryan Texas metropolitan statistical area in general, would fill most of the direct and indirect jobs. However, direct socioeconomic changes because of the proposed project would not be likely, and there would be no changes to population, infrastructure, or the level of social services. In addition, vendors and equipment suppliers would benefit from the purchase of capital and supporting components of the system.

The short duration of these positions would result in a smaller indirect effect than that during 20 or more years of operations.

3.4.2.1.2 *Operations Impacts*

DOE assumed that the proposed project would create six additional direct jobs during operations. These direct jobs would create about four additional indirect jobs for a total of 10 permanent jobs during operations. The Department assumed Texas A&M would hire personnel to operate the facility after design, construction, and installation. The direct jobs would include positions for skilled operations and maintenance individuals and for management personnel. These individuals would be expected to earn about $52,000 annually. The aggregate number of jobs, about 10, would have a small positive impact on the labor force by creating job opportunities that could reduce unemployment and increase labor participation. DOE expects that residents of Brazos County specifically, and residents of the metropolitan statistical area in general, would continue to fill most of the direct and indirect jobs.

In summary, the socioeconomic impacts or consequences of the project include the creation of 600 domestic direct and indirect jobs in the engineering, manufacturing, and construction sectors during the preoperational phase. The project would also create six long-term jobs for operations and management personnel, which would create four indirect jobs. These jobs would stimulate the economic base of the region.

3.4.2.2 No-Action Alternative

The No-Action Alternative would result in no short-term jobs during the construction phase of the project and would create no permanent jobs during operations. In addition, the objectives of the Industrial Technologies Program and the Recovery Act would not be advanced.

3.4.3 ENVIRONMENTAL JUSTICE

Executive Order 12898, "Federal Actions to Address Environmental Justice in Minority Populations and Low-Income Populations," directs federal agencies to address environmental and human health conditions in minority and low-income communities. The evaluation of impacts to environmental justice is dependent on determining if high and adverse impacts from the proposed project would disproportionately affect low-income or minority populations in the affected community.

DOE has determined that direct socioeconomic impacts, other than domestic job creation and the related increase in spending from project expenditures, from the proposed project are unlikely (Section 3.4.2.1). The proposed project likely would not result in workers moving to the area, so there would be no impact to infrastructure including housing and the level of social services in the area. There would be small, positive economic impacts from direct and indirect employment opportunities in the region and increased expenditures of wages.

Table 3-5 lists racial and ethnic data about persons in Brazos County and, for comparison, Texas. In 2008, the aggregate percent of all racial minorities (Black, American Indian or Alaskan Native, Asian, Native Hawaiian or other Native Islander or of two or more races) was 17 percent in Brazos County and 18 percent in Texas. Persons of Hispanic or Latino origin made up 21 percent of the population in Brazos County, much less than the 37 percent in Texas as a whole. Hispanics may be of any race, so are included in applicable race categories. Neither racial nor ethnic minority persons would experience adverse socioeconomic impacts from the proposed projects. There would be small direct socioeconomic impacts to all populations, and the indirect impacts would be small and positive. The economic impacts from the project would include employment opportunities in the region and enhanced final output because of the infusion of project-related spending.

DOE has also determined that there would be no high and adverse impact to low-income populations. In 2008, about 25 percent of the residents in Brazos County lived below the poverty level, and the statewide rate was about 16 percent. There would be small direct socioeconomic impacts to all populations, and the indirect impacts would be small and positive. The economic

Table 3-5. 2008 racial and ethnic characteristics, Brazos County and Texas.

Racial and ethnic characteristics	Brazos County (percent)	Texas (percent)
White	83.1	82.4
Black	10.7	11.9
American Indian and Alaska Native	0.4	0.8
Asian	4.5	3.5
Hawaiian/Other Native Islander	0.1	0.1
Persons reporting two or more races	1.2	1.3
Aggregate minority races	16.9	17.6
Persons of Hispanic or Latino origin[a]	21	36.5

Source: Bureau of the Census 2010a.

a. Includes jobs created by total project expenditures including federal and nonfederal dollars.

impacts from the project would include indirect employment opportunities in the region and enhanced final output as a result of the infusion of project-related spending.

In summary, DOE determined that no high and adverse impacts would occur to any member of the community. Therefore, there would be no adverse and disproportionate impacts to minority or low-income populations.

3.5 Resource Commitments

3.5.1 RELATIONSHIP BETWEEN SHORT-TERM USES OF THE ENVIRONMENT AND THE MAINTENANCE AND ENHANCEMENT OF LONG-TERM PRODUCTIVITY

The installation and operation of a CHP system on the College Station campus would result in short-term uses of land. In this context, *short-term use* of resources means the operating life of the Central Utility Plant and *long-term productivity* refers to the period after the plant has ceased operation and undergone decommissioning and demolition. At that time, the land could be occupied and used for other purposes, or it could be reclaimed and revegetated to resemble conditions that are more natural.

3.6.2 IRREVERSIBLE AND IRRETRIEVABLE COMMITMENTS OF RESOURCES

The use of land as a resource to support the installation and operation of the proposed CHP system would be irretrievable in the short term. Some unrecyclable construction materials, energy, and the fuel for construction and operation would be irreversible and irretrievable commitments of resources. DOE would also have expended funding for the proposed project.

3.6.3 UNAVOIDABLE ADVERSE IMPACTS

The proposed CHP system would result in the unavoidable small adverse impacts of generating air pollutants and small quantities of waste and wastewater. The small unavoidable impacts would be offset by the positive impact of the conversion of waste energy to electricity and steam. This could result in reduced emissions from conventional fossil-fuel generating facilities. There would be short-term increases in noise during construction.

4. CUMULATIVE IMPACTS

Cumulative impacts result from the incremental effects the proposed project could have in combination with the impacts of past, present, and reasonably foreseeable actions. Texas A&M's proposed project would construct and operate a high-efficiency CHP plant on its College Station campus. The primary site is the existing Central Utility Plant. The University has been growing since the 1870s, increasing the campus footprint to about 8,000 acres. The environmental impacts of past actions have already passed through the environment or are captured as part of the current baseline conditions. The affected environment descriptions, which form the existing baseline conditions for comparison to the incremental impacts of the proposed project, include air emissions, water use, waste generation, and socioeconomics (Sections 3.1 to 3.4). The proposed site offers sufficient access and infrastructure to accommodate the plant. For most environmental resource areas, there would be no incremental impacts or the impacts would be small, temporary, or both (Section 1.4).

The following paragraphs describe present and reasonably foreseeable actions in the Brazos County area that could have cumulative impacts in combination with the proposed CHP project.

Natural Gas Pipeline. As an additional utility infrastructure upgrade, Texas A&M is installing a natural gas pipeline on campus along the south side of University Drive southwest from the intersection of Texas Avenue and University Drive to Ireland Street and then into the Central Utility Plant compound. The distance is about 1 mile and the pipeline should be complete by the end of this year; the route would be bored or trenched along existing roadways and installed underground. The new natural gas line would be a replacement upgrade to supply gas at the higher pressure necessary for the new gas turbine. The new line would supply all natural gas needs at the Central Utility Plant. The pipeline work, in conjunction with the electrical duct installation activities, would result in cumulative impacts to campus traffic flow and parking space availability. The University has mitigated these impacts through open communication with the student body, faculty, and staff about times and locations of road and parking lot closures. These impacts would be short term.

Campus Construction. At present the University lists over 40 ongoing or planned projects for the College Station campus (TAMU 2010). The existing and proposed projects total into the hundreds of million dollars and would result in beneficial direct and indirect socioeconomic impacts. The projects include the construction of major classroom buildings, research centers, student housing, upgrades and expansion of existing facilities, and new and upgraded athletic venues. Some of these projects would cumulatively alter existing land use within the campus boundary by using currently vacant land. The projects could affect campus traffic flow and parking space availability. With the exception of the proposed CHP project, most impacts would be limited to the construction period in that, once operational, there would be no air emissions and water use would be of a domestic nature. Some of the new or expanded research laboratories could involve nuclear or hazardous materials. The University would manage these materials to its existing University policies along with State of Texas and federal regulations.

Research Valley. The Research Valley Innovation Center (Research Valley) is a Texas business initiative in the region centered around Brazos County, Texas, the cities of Bryan and College Station, and the Texas A&M University System. Research Valley is focused on science and technology startups. It was formed in May 2007 by the Research Valley Partnership, a public-private economic development corporation, the Texas A&M University System Office of Technology Commercialization, the Texas A&M Health Science Center, and Texas A&M University. Services include management consulting, business plan development, access to a regional service provider network, and physical incubator space. The Research Valley park totals about 1,000 acres. The park could provide cumulative socioeconomic benefits to the local economy. Regional need for infrastructure and utilities could increase. It is expected that any businesses locating at the park, especially those that might include use of radioactive or hazardous materials, would operate in a manner consistent with state and federal regulations.

Easterwood Airport. Texas A&M owns and operates Easterwood Airport, which at present is the only airport in the Bryan-College Station area and the only facility in Research Valley. Easterwood is a regional airport with scheduled commercial airline services and general aviation facilities. Currently listed airport-related projects include Easterwood Airport Taxiway H, Airport High Mast Lighting Improvements, General Aviation Ramp Rehabilitation, New East Side Aviation Apron, and Rehabilitate Runway 10/28. The projects would cumulatively contribute to the benefit the local economy and transportation infrastructure.

Cities of College Station and Bryan. The College Station-Bryan Metropolitan Statistical Area is the eighth fastest growing community in the United States. Growth is projected to extend through 2025 with associated growth in residential and commercial development. The cumulative impacts of this growth would include the loss of vacant land and need to expand utility services and infrastructure. In addition, expansion could put pressure on social services such as medical care, schools, and fire and police services.

5. CONCLUSIONS

Texas A&M proposes to install and operate a high-efficiency CHP system at its campus in College Station, Texas, which occupies about 8,000 acres. The university would install the equipment within the boundaries of its existing Central Utility Plant, install about 2 miles of underground concrete-encased electrical ducts, and upgrade four switching stations.

In this EA, DOE considered:

1. The proposed action of providing a Recovery Act financial assistance grant in a cost-sharing arrangement with Texas A&M,

2. Texas A&M's proposed project, and

3. The No-Action Alternative.

The analyses for this EA considered all the environmental resource areas DOE typically includes in NEPA documents. For most of the environmental resource areas were not carried forward for more detailed analysis because DOE determined there would be no impacts or the potential impacts would be small or temporary in nature, or both (Table 1-1). As a consequence, DOE focused its detailed analyses on those resource areas that would require new or amended permits, have the potential for significant impacts or controversy, or would typically interest the public, such as socioeconomics. These resource areas included:

- Air quality,
- Water resources,
- Waste, and
- Socioeconomics and environmental justice.

In addition, DOE consulted with the Texas State Historic Preservation Officer as required by Section 106 of the National Historic Preservation Act. The Department determined there would be no historic properties affected (see Appendix B).

DOE also reviewed the list of federally threatened and endangered species and their habitat requirements in Brazos County, Texas. The Department determined there would be no effect on federally listed threatened, endangered, or candidate species. DOE sent a consultation letter to the FWS under Section 7 of the Endangered Species Act (see Appendix B).

The proposed project would potentially have beneficial impacts from recovering waste energy and converting it into electricity and steam for use on the campus. This would allow Texas A&M to purchase less electricity from regional power plants, which could reduce pollutant emissions from conventional generating sources that use fossil fuels.

Air Quality. Air emissions during construction for the proposed project on the College Station campus would include combustion emissions from vehicles and heavy-duty equipment and fugitive dust from site preparation activities. These emissions would have short-term adverse impacts that Texas A&M could mitigate through best management practices such as soil stabilization and watering of exposed soils. Fugitive dust emissions would cease on completion of construction, so long-term impacts would be negligible.

Operation of the proposed CHP system would increase some of the Central Utility Plant emissions (PM_{10}, sulfur dioxide, and volatile organic compounds). These emissions could be offset by reductions in emissions at other fossil-fuel electric plants because Texas A&M would purchase significantly less electricity from the regional grid. Emission of carbon monoxide would be lower, and emission of nitrogen oxides would be much lower. Texas A&M would install 45 megawatts of power-generating capacity and reduce the University's carbon dioxide emissions.

Water Resources. The College Station campus is located in the Brazos River watershed. The river lies about eight miles west of campus. There are no surface water bodies at the Central Utility Plant or along the routes for electrical work. The closest water bodies are ponds on the campus golf course.

The proposed project would use groundwater from four local aquifers. During construction, Texas A&M would use appropriate erosion control and storm water management measures to reduce the impacts of erosion and increased runoff under its general construction storm water permit. During operations, the University would discharge wastewater after treatment to its current storm water system, which drains to the Brazos River through several tributaries. The main source of wastewater would be from boiler blowdown, which contains carbonates and scaling materials. The proposed project would have a small impact on the quantity of wastewater the University discharges, and there would be no change in the quality of that wastewater. The current Texas A&M industrial discharge permit would not require modification. Impacts to groundwater availability and quality would be unlikely from normal operations. The University would prevent or mitigate potential impacts from accidental spills of contaminants by following a spill prevention and mitigation plan.

None of the proposed construction activities would occur in a 100-year floodplain, and there are no wetlands in the proposed project areas, so there would be no impacts to floodplains and wetlands.

Waste. Construction for the proposed project would generate construction-related debris such as wood, metal, and concrete. Texas A&M would recycle some of this waste and ship the remainder to a permitted commercial landfill. During normal operations, Texas A&M would generate miscellaneous municipal wastes (for example, wood, paper, garbage, and absorbents) and a minor amount of hazardous waste (aqueous ammonia and metal catalyst) that would not affect regional landfills or treatment plants.

Socioeconomics and Environmental Justice. The proposed project would have the beneficial impact of creating new direct and indirect jobs during construction and operations and stimulating the economic base of the community. DOE expects that members of the community's existing labor force would fill the new jobs, so there would be no adverse impacts to the existing infrastructure or social services. In relation to environmental justice, there would be no adverse and disproportionate impacts to minority and low-income populations because there would be no high and adverse impacts to any member of the community.

Cumulative impact considerations included additional utilities work such as a new natural gas pipeline, College Station campus construction projects, the Research Valley Innovation Center, and projects at the Easterwood Airport. These projects would contribute cumulative short-term impacts to traffic but would also have beneficial socioeconomic impacts. In addition, DOE considered the rapid growth of the College Station-Bryan Metropolitan Statistical Area. The cumulative impacts of this growth would include the loss of vacant land and the need to expand utility services and infrastructure. In addition, expansion could put pressure on social services such as medical care, schools, and fire and police services.

In terms of the No-Action Alternative, DOE assumed Texas A&M would not proceed with the project without DOE assistance; therefore, there would be no impacts to any resource category. However, the above-described potential for positive impacts to air quality and socioeconomics would also not occur. In addition, DOE's ability to achieve its objectives under the Industrial Technologies Program and the Recovery Act would be impaired.

6. REFERENCES

BEA (Bureau of Economic Analysis), 2010a, "Table CA25N-Total full-time and part-time employment by NAICS industry, Brazos County, Texas, 2008," U.S. Department of Commerce, Washington, D.C., April 22, accessed May 12, 2010. http://www.bea.gov/regional/reis/

BEA (Bureau of Economic Analysis), 2010b, "Table CA1-3 Per Capita Personal Income, Texas, 2008," U.S. Department of Commerce, Washington, D.C., April 22, accessed May 12, 2010. http://www.bea.gov/regional/reis/

BLS (Bureau of Labor Statistics), 2009, "Table 1: Incidence Rates - Detailed Industry Level - 2008," U. S. Department of Labor, Washington, D.C., October 29, accessed March 29, 2010. http://www.bls.gov/iif/oshwc/osh/os/ostb2071.txt OS TB 10/29/2009

BLS (Bureau of Labor Statistics), 2010, "Local Area Unemployment Statistics, Brazos County, Texas and Texas, 2009-2010" U.S. Department of Labor, Washington, D.C., accessed May 12 and June 7, 2010. http://data.bls.gov/cgi-bin/dsrv

Bureau of the Census, 2003, "County to County Worker Flow Files for Texas, Sorted by Workplace State and County," Washington, D.C., March 6, accessed May 12 and June 7, 2010. http://www.census.gov/population/www/cen2000/commuting/index.html.

Bureau of the Census, 2010a, "State and County QuickFacts, Texas, College Station Texas, and Brazos County, Texas," Washington, D.C., April 22, accessed May 12, 2010. http://quickfacts.census.gov/

Bureau of the Census, 2010b, "Table 1. Annual Estimates of the Population of Metropolitan and Micropolitan Statistical Areas: April 1, 2000 to July 1, 2009," Washington, D.C., March, accessed June 1, 2010. http://factfinder.census.gov/.

DOE (U.S. Department of Energy), 2000, *Clean Air Act General Conformity Requirements and the National Environmental Policy Act Process*, Office of Environment, Safety and Health, Washington, D.C., April.

FWS (U.S. Fish and Wildlife Service), 2010, "Endangered Species List, List of Species by County for Texas: Counties Selected: Brazos, Southwest Regional Office, Albuquerque, New Mexico, accessed June 23, 2010. http://www.fws.gov/southwest/es/EndangeredSpecies/lists/ListSpecies.cfm

Hightower, C. S., 2010a, "Texas A-M Preliminary Draft EA - TAMU Revisions 7_13_2010," e-mail to B. Craig (Dade Moeller & Associates), Texas A&M University, College Station, Texas, July 13.

Hightower, C. S., 2010b, "TAMU CHP Environmental Assessment Information," e-mail to B. Craig (Dade Moeller & Associates), Texas A&M University, College Station, Texas, June 4.

Hightower, C. S., 2010c, "FW: RE: DOE Environmental Assessment Information," e-mail to B. Craig (Dade Moeller & Associates), Texas A&M University, College Station, Texas, June 18.

Inman, A. M., 2010, untitled letter to J. G. Riley (Texas A&M University), Texas Commission on Environmental Quality, Austin, Texas, February 10.

IPCC (Intergovernmental Panel on Climate Change), 2007, *Climate Change 2007: Synthesis Report, Summary for Policy Makers*, Geneva, Switzerland.

McAnally, C. K., 2010, "RE: DOE Environmental Assessment Information," e-mail to D. Petersen (Texas A&M University), Jacobs Engineering, June 21.

Nelson, J., 2010, "CHP Major Plant Equipment," Texas A&M University, College Station, Texas, May 20, accessed June 11, 2010. http://utilities.tamu.edu/index.php?option=com_content&view=article&id=51

Riley, J. G., 2009, "U.S. Department of Energy Environmental Questionnaire," Texas A&M University, College Station, Texas, July 13.

Riley, J. G., 2010, "Combined Heat and Power (CHP) Project," Texas A&M University, College Station, Texas, May 19, accessed June 9, 2010. http://utilities.tamu.edu/index.php?option=com_content&view=article&id=49

TAMU (Texas A&M University), 2009, *Project Narrative and Project Management Plan, DE-FOA-0000044, Area 1 - Texas A&M University Combined Heat and Power System*, College Station, Texas.

TAMU (Texas A&M University), 2010, "Facilities Planning & Construction, The Texas A&M University System," College Station, Texas, accessed June 22, 2010. http://www.tamus.edu/offices/fpc/projects.html

TAMU (Texas A&M University), undated, "Occupational Safety," College Station, Texas, accessed June 21. http://ehsd.tamu.edu/OccupationalSafety.aspx

APPENDIX A
DISTRIBUTION LIST

Mr. Toby Baker
Governor's Advisor – Natural Resources and Agriculture
P.O. Box 12428
Austin, Texas 78711

The Honorable Nancy Berry
Mayor of College Station
1101 Texas Avenue
College Station, Texas 77840

The Honorable Jason Bienski
Mayor of Bryan
300 South Texas Avenue
Bryan, Texas 77803

The Honorable Fred Brown
Texas House of Representatives
P.O. Box 2910
Austin, Texas 78768

Dr. Russell Cross
Texas A&M University
401 Joe Routt Blvd
MS 1179 TAMU
College Station, Texas 77843

The Honorable Chet Edwards
U.S. House of Representatives
4001 East 29th Street, Suite 116
Bryan, Texas 77802

Ms. Denise Stines Francis
State Single Point of Contact
Governor's Office of Budget, Planning, and Policy; State Grants Team
P.O. Box 12428
Austin, Texas 78711

Mr. Kevin Haggerty
U.S. Department of Energy
Freedom of Information Act Reading Room
1000 Independence Avenue, SW, 1-G-033
Washington, D.C. 20585

Ms. Lallah Howard
Texas A&M University
MS 1247 TAMU
College Station, Texas 77843-1247

Mr. Michael P. Jansky
Regional Environmental Review Coordinator
Office of Planning and Coordination
U.S. Environmental Protection Agency
1445 Ross Avenue, Mail Code 6EN-XP
Dallas, Texas 75202-2733

Mr. Bowen Loftin
President Texas A&M University
401 Joe Routt Boulevard
MS 1246 TAMU
College Station, Texas 77843

Mr. Mike McKinney
Chancellor, Texas A&M University
200 Technology Way, Suite 2043
College Station, Texas 77845

The Honorable Steve Ogden
Texas State Senate
P.O. Box 12068
Austin, Texas 78711-2068

Mr. Steve Parris
U.S. Fish and Wildlife Service
Clean Lake Ecological Services Field Office
17629 El Camino Real, Suite 211
Houston, Texas 77058

The Honorable Rick Perry
Governor of Texas
Office of the Governor
P.O. Box 12428
Austin, Texas 78711-2428

Mr. James G. Riley
Director, Utilities and Energy Management
1581 TAMU
College Station, Texas 77843-1584

Texas Commission on Environmental Quality
5425 Polk Ave Suite H
Houston, Texas 77023

Texas Department of Licensing and Regulation
P.O. Box 12157
Austin, Texas 78711

Mr. Mark Wolfe
State Historic Preservation Officer
Texas Historical Commission
P.O. Box 12276
Austin, Texas 78711

Mr. Terry Zrubek
Governor's Advisor – Water
P.O. Box 12428
Austin, Texas 78711

APPENDIX B
CONSULTATIONS

This appendix contains copies of:

- The consultation letter from DOE to the Texas State Historic Preservation Officer (page B-2),
- The reply from the Texas State Historic Preservation Officer to DOE (p. B-15), and
- The informational letter from DOE to the FWS (page B-16).

 **NATIONAL ENERGY TECHNOLOGY LABORATORY**
Albany, OR · Morgantown, WV · Pittsburgh, PA

 U.S. DEPARTMENT OF
ENERGY

July 1, 2010

Mr. Mark Wolfe
State Historic Preservation Officer
Texas Historical Commission
P.O. Box 12276
Austin, Texas 78711

RE: U.S. Department of Energy Request for Consultation on the Texas A&M University Combined Heat and Power Project, College Station, Texas

Dear Mr. Wolfe:

The U.S. Department of Energy (DOE or the Department) proposes to provide a financial assistance grant to Texas A&M University (the University) through the Industrial Energy Efficiency Initiative of the American Reinvestment and Recovery Act (Recovery Act). Funding to the University would be used to install a new high-efficiency combined heat and power system to supply energy, heating, and cooling needs to the University's College Station campus. The system would be installed at 498 Ireland Street, College Station, Brazos County, Texas.

To comply with Section 106 of the National Historic Preservation Act, DOE has evaluated the potential impacts of the proposed project and determined that no historic properties would be affected. In accordance with the implementing regulations of the Act at 36 CFR Part 800, DOE is providing you with documentation of that finding in the form of a completed *Application for Request for SHPO Consultation*, along with maps and photographs.

DOE will be issuing a draft environmental assessment (EA) on this subject within the next few weeks for public review and comment. A copy of the EA will be sent to your office. Correspondence between your office and DOE will also be included in an appendix to the EA.

Please forward any request for additional information or clarification to Mr. Bill Gwilliam of the Department's National Energy Technology Laboratory using the contact information in the application.

Since this is an American Recovery and Reinvestment Act project, we would appreciate a quick response to DOE's request for consultation.

Thank you in advance your consideration.

Sincerely,

Bill Gwilliam
NEPA Document Manager

Enclosure

TEXAS HISTORICAL COMMISSION

REQUEST FOR SHPO CONSULTATION:
Projects Subject to Section 106 of the National Historic Preservation Act
and/or the Antiquities Code of Texas

Submission of this form only initiates consultation with the Texas Historical Commission, the State Historic Preservation Officer (SHPO) for Texas. The SHPO may require additional information to complete the review for some projects.

FCC projects: this form should not be completed when submitting Form 620 or 621 for communications towers.

Section 106 of the National Historic Preservation Act of 1966, as amended, requires federal agencies to consider the effects of their undertakings on historic properties and to consult with the State Historic Preservation Officer (SHPO) regarding the undertaking. An undertaking is any action by or on behalf of a federal agency that has the potential to affect historic resources and includes funding, permits, or other approvals. Federal agencies are required to identify historic resources that may be affected and to avoid, minimize, or mitigate any adverse effects. The Section 106 regulations are codified in 36 CFR 800 and are available from the Advisory Council on Historic Preservation website at www.achp.gov. Regulations allow 30 days upon receipt for SHPO review.

The Antiquities Code of Texas (Title 9, Chapter 191 of the Texas Natural Resources Code) is intended to protect historic and archeological landmarks and is applicable to public lands owned by the state of Texas or a political subdivision of the state, including state agencies, counties, cities, school districts, and public colleges and universities, as well as other public authorities. Notification of the Texas Historical Commission is required before breaking ground at a project location on state or local public land.

☑ **This is a new submission**
Complete all pages of this form and include required attachments.

☐ **This is additional information relating to original submission made on or about** _____
Complete only the first page of this form and add any new information, including attachments.

1. Project Information

PROJECT NAME
Texas A&M University Combined Heat and Power Project, College Station, Texas

PROJECT ADDRESS	PROJECT CITY	PROJECT ZIP CODE(S)
498 Ireland Street	College Station	77843-1584

PROJECT COUNTY OR COUNTIES
Brazos

PROJECT TYPE (Check all that apply)

☐ Road/Highway Construction or Improvement   ☑ Repair, Rehabilitation or Renovation of Structure(s)
☑ Site Excavation   ☐ Addition to Existing Structure(s)
☑ Utilities & Infrastructure   ☐ Demolition or Relocation of Existing Structure(s)
☑ New Construction   ☐ None of these

BRIEF PROJECT SUMMARY: Please provide a one or two sentence description to explain the project. More details will be provided separately in Part 5, the Project Work Description Attachment.

DOE is proposing to provide Texas A&M partial funding to install and operate a high-efficiency combined heat and power system within the University's existing Central Utility Plant.

2. Project Contact Information

PROJECT CONTACT NAME	TITLE	ORGANIZATION
Bill Gwilliam	NEPA Document Manager	U.S. Department of Energy

ADDRESS	CITY	STATE	ZIP
3610 Collins Ferry Road, P.O. Box 880 MS B07	Morgantown	West Virginia	26507-0888

PHONE	EMAIL
304-285-4401	william.gwilliam@netl.doe.gov

For SHPO Use Only
Track Review to:

☐ Archeology Division: Reviewer:

☐ History Programs Division: Reviewer:

☐ Architecture Division: Reviewer:

Date Stamp Below:

3

3. Federal Involvement

Does this project involve approval, permit, license, or funding from a federal agency?

☑ Yes (Please complete this section) ☐ No (Skip to next box)

FEDERAL AGENCY
U.S. Department of Energy

FEDERAL PROGRAM, FUNDING, OR PERMIT TYPE
American Recovery and Reinvestment Act Industrial Energy Efficiency Program

FEDERAL AGENCY CONTACT PERSON
Bill Gwilliam

PHONE
304-285-4401

ADDRESS
3610 Collins Ferry Road, P.O. Box 880 MS B07 West Virginia 26507-0888

EMAIL
william.gwilliam@netl.doe.gov

Has the federal agency (if other than HUD) formally delegated authority to consult with SHPO on the agency's behalf? ☐ Yes (Please attach delegation letter) ☑ No

4. State Involvement

Does this project involve approval, permit, license, or funding from a state agency?

☑ Yes (Please complete this section) ☐ No (Skip to next box)

STATE AGENCY
See attachment

STATE PROGRAM, FUNDING, OR PERMIT TYPE
Funding as an institution within the state university system

STATE AGENCY CONTACT PERSON

PHONE

ADDRESS

EMAIL

Will this project involve public land owned by the State of Texas or a political subdivision of the state? (State Agency, County, City, School District, Public Authority, Public College or University, etc.)

☑ Yes ☐ No

CURRENT OR FUTURE OWNER OF THE PUBLIC LAND
Texas A&M University, College Station, Texas

5. Project Work Description

Attach a detailed written description of the project that fully explains what will be constructed, altered, or demolished. Include architectural or engineering plans, site plans, specifications, or NEPA documents, as necessary, to illustrate the project.

6. Identification of Project Location and Area of Potential Effect (APE)

The APE includes the entire area within which historic properties could be affected by the project. This includes all areas of construction, demolition, and ground disturbance (direct effects) and the broader surrounding area that might experience visual or other effects from the project (indirect effects).

1. **Attach** map(s) indicating the location and specific boundaries of the project. Road names must be included and legible. Identify the project location, boundaries, and APE on the map(s) as precisely as possible. Suggested maps may include USGS 7.5 minute quadrangle maps (or relevant portions thereof), tax maps, satellite images, etc. The number and types of map(s) will depend on the nature and complexity of the project as well as the extent of the APE. **Projects involving ground disturbance must include the appropriate 7.5 minute USGS quadrangle.**

2. **Attach** a brief written description of the APE, including a discussion of the potential for direct and indirect effects that might result from the project and the justification for the boundaries chosen for the APE.

PROJECT NAME
Texas A&M University Combined Heat and Power Project, College Station, Texas

VER 0110

4

7. Identification of Historic Properties within the APE (Attach additional materials as necessary)

A. Archeological Resources

Does this project involve ground-disturbing activity?

■ Yes (Please complete this section)　　□ No (Skip to Structures section)

Describe the nature, width, length, and depth of the proposed ground-disturbing activity
See Attachment

Describe previous land use and disturbances:
The site has been used for generating electricity and steam since 1893.

Describe the current land use and conditions
The land is part of the existing Central Utility Plant, it a heavily industrialized area in the process of upgrading its power generating and steam equipment.

B. Structures

Are there any structures, buildings, or designed landscape features (park, cemetery, etc.) 45 years old or older within the project area or APE?

■ Yes　　　　　　　　　　　□ No

Is the project located within or adjacent to a district that is listed in or eligible for the National Register of Historic Places? Eligible districts may include locally designated districts or areas identified in historic resource surveys
□ Yes, name of district _____　　□ No　　　　■ Do not know

If the Texas Historic Sites Atlas (http://atlas.thc.state.tx.us) has been consulted, were previously identified architectural resources identified within the project area or APE?
□ Yes　　　　　　　　■ No　　　　　　□ Did not consult Atlas

If the answer to any of the above questions is yes, use the space below or provide an attachment identifying each structure, building, designed landscape feature, or district within the APE that is 45 years old or older. Include an actual or estimated date of construction and the location of each of the features.
See Attachment

Does the project involve the rehabilitation, alteration, removal, or demolition of any structure, building, designed landscape feature, or district that is 45 years old or older?

■ Yes　　　　　　　　　　　□ No

If yes, include information with the attachments for Part 5: Project Work Description and Part 8: Photographs.

8. Photographs

Attach clear, high-resolution color photographs that illustrate the project area and APE as defined in Section 6. Images from the internet are not acceptable due to low resolution. Photography should document the project area and properties within the APE, including clear views of any buildings or structures. Please number and label all photographs, and include a map or site plan labeled to show the location and direction of each view. Where applicable, include photographs of the surrounding area from the project site and streetscape images. Should your project entail the alteration of existing structures, please also provide photographs of the existing conditions of sites, buildings, and exterior and interior areas to be affected.

9. Consulting Parties/Public Notification (Section 106 only)

Attach a description of the actions taken to notify the public or invite consultation with parties other than SHPO. Provide a summary of any consultation and comments received from consulting parties or the public.

The SHPO is only one consulting party under Section 106. Refer to 36 CFR 800.2 for information about other participants who are entitled to comment on the Section 106 process, including Native American tribes, interested parties, and the public. Consultation with the SHPO is not a substitution for consultation with Native American tribes. When identifying historic resources within the APE and determining the effect of an undertaking, applicants should consider consulting with the county historical commission and the local historic preservation officer, if any.

PROJECT NAME	
	Texas A&M University Combined Heat and Power Project, College Station, Texas

VER 0110

5

10. Applicant's Determination of Effect (Section 106 only)

An effect occurs when an action alters the characteristics of a property that qualify it for listing in the National Register of Historic Places, including changes to the property's location, design, setting, materials, workmanship, feeling, and association. Effects can be direct or indirect, and can be physical, visual, audible, or economic. They may include a change in ownership or change in use.

☒ **No Historic Properties Affected** based on 36 CFR 800.4(d)(1). Please provide the basis for this determination.

☐ **No Adverse Effect** on historic properties based on 36 CFR 800.5(b). Please explain why the criteria of adverse effect at 36 CFR 800.5(a)(1) were not found to be applicable for your project.

☐ **Adverse Effect** on historic properties based on 36 CFR 800.5(d)(2). Please explain why the criteria of adverse effect at 36 CFR 800.5(a)(1) were found to be applicable to your project. You may also wish to include an explanation of how these adverse effects might be avoided, minimized, or mitigated.

In the space below or as an attachment, please explain the effect of the project on historic properties.

See Attachment.

Submit Completed Form and Attachments to:

Via mail:
Mark Wolfe
State Historic Preservation Officer
Texas Historical Commission
PO Box 12276
Austin, TX 78711

Via hand delivery or private express delivery:
Mark Wolfe
State Historic Preservation Officer
Texas Historical Commission
108 West 16th St.
Austin, TX 78701

Faxes and email are not acceptable.

For SHPO Use Only

PROJECT NAME		
Texas A&M University Combined Heat and Power Project, College Station, Texas		
PROJECT ADDRESS	PROJECT CITY	PROJECT ZIP CODE(S)
495 Ireland Street	College Station	77843-1584
PROJECT COUNTY OR COUNTIES		
Brazos		
PROJECT CONTACT NAME	TITLE	ORGANIZATION
Bill Gwilliam	NEPA Document Manager	U.S. Department of Energy
ADDRESS	CITY	STATE	ZIP
3610 Collins Ferry Road P.O. Box 880 MS 807	Morgantown	West Virginia	26507-0888
PHONE	EMAIL	
304-285-4401	william.gwilliam@netl.doe.gov	

VER 0110

6

Attachment
Request for SHPO Consultation
4. State Involvement
Texas Commission on Environmental Quality – Air Quality Permit
Texas Department of Licensing and Registration – Boiler Registration

5. Project Work Description

The U.S. Department of Energy (DOE or the Department) is proposing to provide a financial assistance grant to Texas A&M University (the University) for the installation and operation of a combined heat and power system at the University's existing Central Utility Plant (CUP) with associated electrical duct bank and switching station work.

The proposed project would require the construction of foundations and enclosures for a 34-megawatt natural gas combustion turbine and a 210,000-pound-per-hour heat recovery steam generator. The University would also install an 11-megawatt steam turbine generator in an existing building. The project would include associated operating equipment and piping between new and existing CUP equipment.

The project would involve the following:

- The new equipment would be tied-in to and use the existing cooling towers;

- Retiring two steam turbine generators, one gas turbine, one boiler, and one heat recovery steam generator;

- Upgrading an existing boiler;

- Installing new electrical duct banks;

- Upgrading switching station switchgear.

- Laying a new foundation for the new 34-megawatt gas turbine and auxiliary equipment;

- Constructing a new foundation and structure to house the new heat recovery steam generator; and/

- Refurbishing an existing building to house the new 11-megawatt steam turbine generator.

Figure 1 is an aerial view of the site and shows the locations for the new equipment.

6. Identification of the Project Area and the Area of Potential Effects

Figure 2 is the U.S. Geological Survey Wellborn, Texas, 7.5-minute quadrangle (2010) showing the location of the Area of Potential Effects (APE) within the bolded lines. Figure 3 shows the CUP with surrounding street names

7

Work for the federally funded portion of the project would occur within the existing CUP and at the routes for duct bank and switching station work, which DOE defines as the Area of Potential Effects (APE).

In relation to secondary effects on nearby properties, DOE has determined that the visual characteristics of the APE would remain essentially the same. There would not be major changes in the appearance of buildings within the CUP. The size of the CUP would not be expanded and the new equipment and associated enclosures would not vary in appearance from existing equipment. In relation to noise, the noise level of the new equipment is rated by the vendor to be less than 85 A-weighted decibels at 3 feet. Given the distance to the nearest receptors outside the CUP, noise would levels would not appreciably exceed ambient levels.

7.A. Archeological Resources

Primary ground disturbance would occur within the CUP for construction of new foundations and equipment enclosures. Most areas within the CUP not hosting buildings have been previously disturbed, including the demolition of buildings and foundations. In addition, the University would install about 2 miles of underground concrete-encased electrical ducts (Figure 4). This work would involve trenching along existing roadways and would cross the University's drill field. Four switching stations would also be installed—two on the west side of Wellborn Road, one at the CUP, and one in the basement of Heldenfels Hall.

7. Identification of Historic Properties within the APE
Part B. Structures

Figure 1 identifies properties in the APE that are at least 45 years old.

9. Consulting Parties/Public Notification

DOE examined the National Park Service Native American Consultation Database and other sources and identified no tribes that might attach religious or cultural significance to historic properties that might exist near the project site. Therefore, the Department has not consulted with any tribes.

DOE is preparing an environmental assessment (EA) to evaluate the impacts of partially funding the Texas A&M University Combined Heat and Power project, including impacts on cultural resources. The availability of the draft EA will be announced in the local newspaper of record, and copies of the EA will be sent to the public library and a distribution list compiled by DOE in cooperation with the University. Through these efforts, DOE will solicit public review and comment.

10. Applicant's Determination of Effect

In accordance with the Section 106 review requirement of the National Historic Preservation Act and the provisions of 36 CFR Part 800, DOE has determined that no historic properties will be affected for the following reasons:

8

- All direct impacts of the proposed project would occur within the APE. Changes in the visual characteristics of the site would result in little variation from the existing visual characteristics of the site.

- There are no known historic properties within the APE. DOE is not aware of any Native American tribes that would have interest in this site.

- Noise levels 3-feet from the new equipment would be less than 85 A-weighted decibels and reduce substantially as distance from the source is increased.

9

Figure 1. Locations of buildings over 45 years old in the CUP and new major equipment locations.

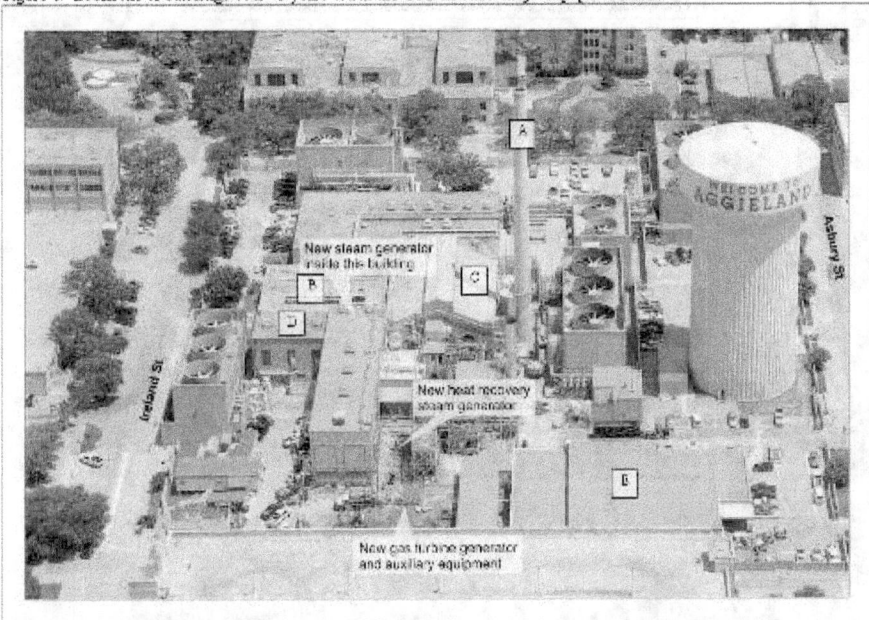

A = Smoke stack, ca. 1940; B = Engine Room, 1917; C = Boiler Room, ca. 1917;
D = Steam Turbine Generator Room, ca. 1950; E = Utility Central Office, over 45 years old.

10

 NATIONAL ENERGY TECHNOLOGY LABORATORY
Albany, OR • Morgantown, WV • Pittsburgh, PA
 U.S. DEPARTMENT OF ENERGY

Figure 2 U.S. Geological Survey Wellborn Quadrangle showing project location

3610 Collins Ferry Road, P.O. Box 880, Morgantown, WV 26507

Figure 3. Satellite view showing Central Utility Plant and equipment location.

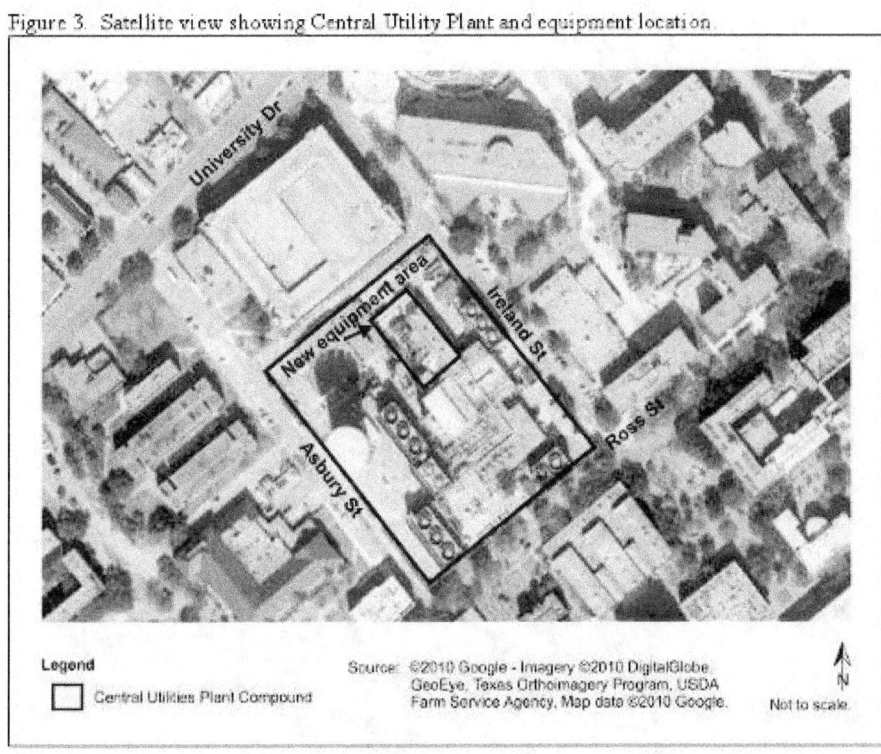

12

Figure 4. Electrical duct bank and switching station work.

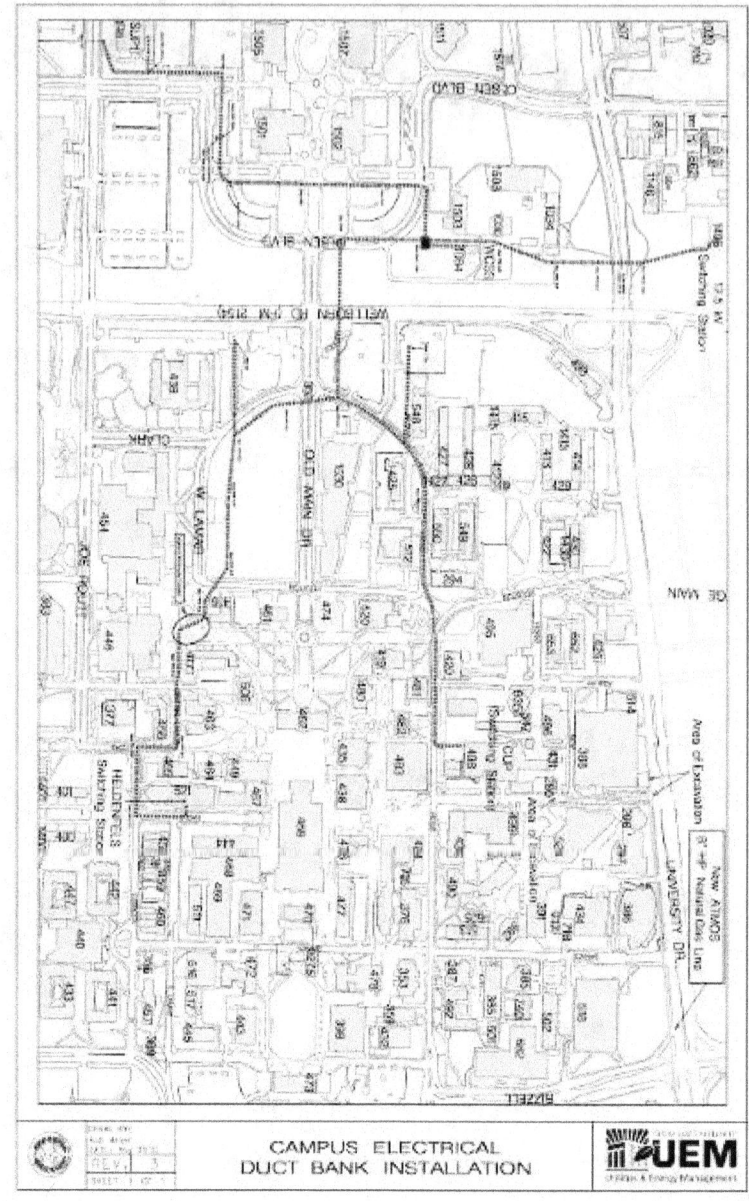

13

NETL NATIONAL ENERGY TECHNOLOGY LABORATORY
Albany, OR · Morgantown, WV · Pittsburgh, PA

U.S. DEPARTMENT OF
ENERGY

July 1, 2010

JUL 07 2010

History Programs Division

Mr. Mark Wolfe
State Historic Preservation Officer
Texas Historical Commission
P.O. Box 12276
Austin, Texas 78711

NO HISTORIC
PROPERTIES AFFECTED
PROJECT MAY PROCEED

RECD JUL 07 2010

by _____
for Mark Wolfe
State Historic Preservation Officer
Date _____

**RE: U.S. Department of Energy Request for Consultation on the Texas A&M University
Combined Heat and Power Project, College Station, Texas**

Dear Mr. Wolfe:

The U.S. Department of Energy (DOE or the Department) proposes to provide a financial
assistance grant to Texas A&M University (the University) through the Industrial Energy
Efficiency Initiative of the American Reinvestment and Recovery Act (Recovery Act). Funding to
the University would be used to install a new high-efficiency combined heat and power system to
supply energy, heating, and cooling needs to the University's College Station campus. The system
would be installed at 498 Ireland Street, College Station, Brazos County, Texas.

To comply with Section 106 of the National Historic Preservation Act, DOE has evaluated the
potential impacts of the proposed project and determined that no historic properties would be
affected. In accordance with the implementing regulations of the Act at 36 CFR Part 800, DOE is
providing you with documentation of that finding in the form of a completed *Application for
Request for SHPO Consultation*, along with maps and photographs.

DOE will be issuing a draft environmental assessment (EA) on this subject within the next few
weeks for public review and comment. A copy of the EA will be sent to your office.
Correspondence between your office and DOE will also be included in an appendix to the EA.

Please forward any request for additional information or clarification to Mr. Bill Gwilliam of the
Department's National Energy Technology Laboratory using the contact information in the
application.

Since this is an American Recovery and Reinvestment Act project, we would appreciate a quick
response to DOE's request for consultation.

 **NATIONAL ENERGY TECHNOLOGY LABORATORY**
Albany, OR · Morgantown, WV · Pittsburgh, PA

 **U.S. DEPARTMENT OF ENERGY**

July 12, 2010

Ms. Edith Erfling
Acting Field Supervisor
U.S. Fish and Wildlife Service
17629 El Camino Real
Suite 211
Houston, TX 77058

RE: Section 7 Review under the Endangered Species Act

Dear Ms. Erfling:

The U.S. Department of Energy (DOE or the Department) is proposing to provide a financial assistance grant to Texas A&M University (Texas A&M or the University) for a proposed project to install and operate a high-efficiency combined heat and power system at its campus at College Station, Texas, in Brazos County.

The proposed project would install and operate a 34-megawatt natural gas turbine generator, a heat recovery steam generator, and an 11-megawatt steam turbine generator at Texas A&M's Central Utility Plant (CUP). These would generate steam for heating and cooling as well as electricity as part of a larger plan to upgrade the University CUP.

The proposed project would primarily occur within the boundaries of the existing CUP, which consists of several buildings and support structures. In addition, Texas A&M would install about two miles of electrical duct banks and upgrade existing switching stations. The electrical duct banks would be installed underground along existing campus roadways and the parade grounds. Figures 1, 2, and 3 shows a satellite view of the College Station Campus and vicinity with the proposed project outlined, the location of the underground duct work, and a close-up showing the area for the new equipment, respectively.

The U.S. Fish and Wildlife Service reports four federally endangered or candidate species that might occur in Brazos County: two endangered species, the Whooping Crane (*Grus Americana*) and Navasota Ladies'-Tresses (*Spiranthes parksii*), along with two candidate species, the Sharpnose Shiner (*Notropus oxyrhynchus*) and Smalleye Shiner (*Notropus buccula*).

DOE reviewed the list of federally threatened, endangered, and candidate species, and their habitat requirements in Brazos County. Due to the location of the proposed facility within the confines of the existing campus and CUP, the Department has determined that there would be no effect on threatened, endangered, or candidate species.

DOE is preparing an environmental assessment (EA) for the proposed project to comply with the requirements of the *National Environmental Policy Act* (NEPA) and the *Section 7 review requirements of the Endangered Species Act.* The EA will be released to the public in the next few weeks and your office will receive a copy. DOE will include all correspondence with the U.S. Fish and Wildlife Service in an appendix to the EA. At this time DOE anticipates a 15-day public comment period for this proposed project.

Please forward the results of your review and any requests for additional information to:

> Mr. Bill Gwilliam
> NEPA Document Manager
> U.S. Department of Energy
> National Energy Technology Laboratory
> P.O. Box 880, MS B07
> 3610 Collins Ferry Road
> Morgantown, West Virginia 26507-0880
> Email: william.gwilliam@netl.doe.gov
> Phone: 304-285-4401

The Department thanks you in advance for your consideration.

Sincerely,

W. S. Gwilliam

Bill Gwilliam
NEPA Document Manager

Figure 1. Satellite view of the College Station campus and vicinity showing the location of the proposed project.
Figure 2. Location of underground electrical duct work.
Figure 3. Central Utility Plant showing area for new equipment.

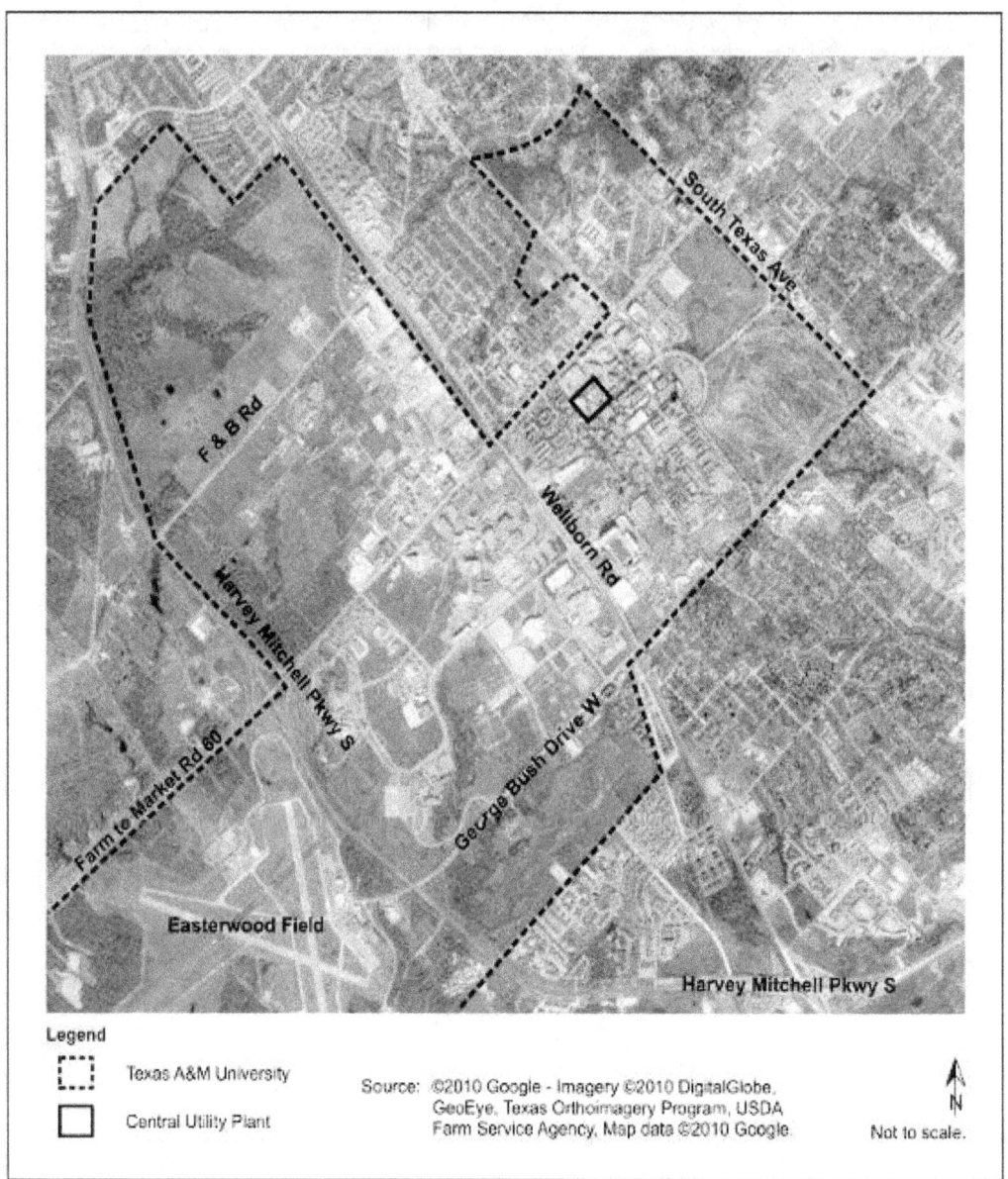

Figure 1. Satellite view of the College Station campus and vicinity showing the location of the proposed project.

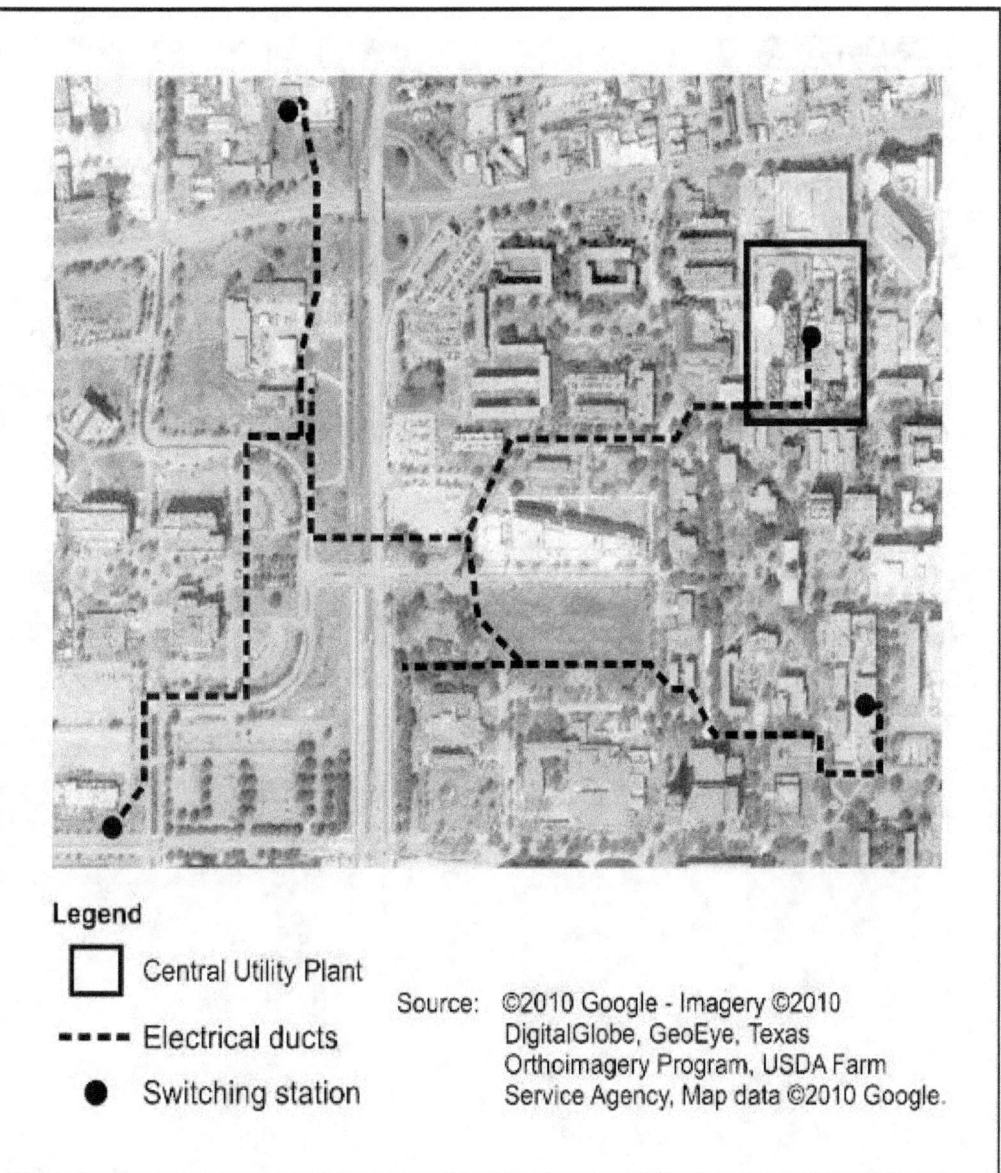

Legend

☐ Central Utility Plant

- - - - Electrical ducts

● Switching station

Source: ©2010 Google - Imagery ©2010 DigitalGlobe, GeoEye, Texas Orthoimagery Program, USDA Farm Service Agency, Map data ©2010 Google.

Figure 2   Location of underground electrical duct work.

Figure 3. Central Utility Plant showing area for new equipment.